Best Practices Under the FCPA and Bribery Act

How to Create a First Class Compliance Program

By

Thomas Fox

Best Practices Under the FCPA and Bribery Act
How to Create a First Class Compliance Program

By Thomas Fox

ISBN-13: 978-1482632453

Contents

ACKNOWLEDGEMENTS

I have been assisted by many people in my journey through FCPA compliance and I want to acknowledge some of them in this volume. Tracy Spears gave me the chance to speak on compliance with both Stephen Martin and Mike Volkov, who not only have been great speaking partners at various events but two compliance practitioners I have learned quite a bit listening to at the events Tracy has sponsored. Bruce Carton, Doug Cornelius and Matt Kelly have all been mentors to me at various stages in my compliance career. Maurice Gilbert has given me the opportunity to be a part of his outstanding team at Corporate Compliance Insights. Matt Ellis and Mary Jones are two folks I am privileged to call colleagues and I have gained experience by working with both of them. Ryan Morgan has been a consistent supporter of my work and has been instrumental in giving me the opportunity to write and speak with. Dan Myers hired me to work at Halliburton and set me off on my in-house career and has been a mentor and with his wife Sonja, good friends to this day. For my Bribery Act insights I have to thank Barry Vitou and Richard Kovalevsky, Q.C. a/k/a 'thebriberyact' guys who not only continue to shed light on the UK compliance law but have helped inform my understanding of the Bribery Act.

And, finally, to my wife Michele who once again not only edited this book but put up with me throughout the process.

FOREWARD

In the current global marketplace, Foreign Corrupt Practices Act ("FCPA") risk needs to be on the radar screen of most companies - large and small, public and private, and across industry sectors. Given the current enforcement theories of the Department of Justice and Securities and Exchange Commission, FCPA risk is not always apparent from reading the statute. There is no way for business organizations to truly eliminate FCPA risk, but such risk can be effectively managed and minimized through pro-active policies and procedures and other means of risk assessment.

Thomas Fox is a leading authority on FCPA compliance and risk assessment and his prior experience as a former corporate counsel gives him a unique perspective in integrating compliance into business strategy. In The Best Practices Under the FCPA and UK Bribery Act, he provides a comprehensive overview of FCPA and Bribery Act compliance and risk assessment and offers best practices that can be put to use from the boardroom to the training room and points in between. Fox's use of real events as learning devices to demonstrate compliance best practices makes this book an engaging and informative read.

Professor Mike Koehler

Founder and Editor of FCPA Professor
(www.fcpaprofessor.com)

INTRODUCTION

Over the past few years I have tried to provide the compliance practitioner with solid information that can be used to implement, review and enhance a US Foreign Corrupt Practices Act (FCPA) or UK Bribery Act based compliance program. I am often asked to collect my blog posting regarding what are the current best practices for an anti-corruption/anti-bribery compliance program. In other words, what are the specifics of a compliance program? This volume is an attempt to provide the compliance practitioner with information that can be used for the *'nuts and bolts'* of compliance.

Using a format similar to the recent US Department of Justice (DOJ) and Securities and Exchange Commission (SEC) guide, *"A Resource Guide to the U.S. Foreign Corrupt Practices Act. The Foreign Corrupt Practices Act (FCPA)"* [the "Guidance"], I have included some of my thoughts on what you can do to create and maintain a best practices compliance program. I have also included some of my prior articles on how to create and maintain such a compliance program using the Six Principles of Adequate Procedures compliance regime under the UK Bribery Act.

I hope that you will find the enclosed useful.

PART I - THE FCPA

1. Commitment from Senior Management and a Clearly Articulated Policy Against Corruption

Introduction

The FCPA Guidance specifies that within a business organization, compliance begins with the board of directors and senior executives setting the proper tone for the rest of the company. Managers and employees take their cues from these corporate leaders. There must be a high-level commitment that is also reinforced and implemented by middle managers and employees at all levels of a business. Therefore, compliance with the FCPA and ethical rules must start at the top. Both the DOJ and SEC evaluate whether senior management has clearly articulated company standards, communicated them in unambiguous terms, adhered to them scrupulously, and disseminated them throughout the organization.

Will No One Rid Me of this Meddlesome Priest?

Posted July 27, 2011

Tone at the Top has become a phrase inculcated in the compliance world. The reason it is so important to any compliance program is because it does actually matter. Any compliance program starts at the top and flows down throughout the company. The concept of appropriate tone at the top is in the US Sentencing Guidelines for organizations accused of violating the Foreign Corrupt Practices Act (FCPA); the Department of Justice's (DOJ) *best practices* for effective compliance programs which have been released with each Deferred Prosecution Agreement (DPA) over the past year; the UK Bribery Act's Six Principles of *Adequate Procedures*; and the OECD Good Practices. The reason all of these guidelines incorporate it into their respective practices is that all employees look to the top of the company to see what is important. Or to quote my colleague Mike Volkov, who quoted Bob Dylan, in opining *"You don't need to be a weatherman to know which way the wind blows"*.

The US Sentencing Guidelines reads:

> High-level personnel and substantial authority personnel of the organization shall be knowledgeable about the content and operation of the compliance and ethics program … and shall promote an organizational culture that encourages ethical conduct and a commitment to compliance with the law.

The OECD *Good Practices* reads:

1. strong, explicit and visible support and commitment from senior management to the company's internal controls, ethics and compliance programs or measures for preventing and detecting foreign bribery;

The UK Bribery Act Guidance for the Six Principles of *Adequate Procedures* reads:

> The top-level management of a commercial organisation (be it a board of directors, the owners or any other equivalent body or person) are committed to preventing bribery by persons associated with it. They foster a culture within the organisation in which bribery is never acceptable.

Attachment C, to each DPA released in the past year, has the following

2. [The Company] will ensure that its senior management provides strong, explicit, and visible support and commitment to its corporate policy against violations of the anti-corruption laws and its compliance code.

The FCPA world is riddled with cases where the abject failure of any ethical "Tone at the Top" led to enforcement actions and large monetary settlements. In the two largest monetary settlements of enforcement actions to date, Siemens and Halliburton, for the actions of its former subsidiary KBR, the government specifically noted the companies' pervasive tolerance for bribery. In the Siemens case, for example, the Securities and Exchange Commission (SEC) noted that the company's culture "had long been at odds with the FCPA" and was one in which bribery "was tolerated and even rewarded at the highest levels". Likewise, in the KBR case, the government noted that "tolerance of the offense by substantial authority personnel was pervasive" throughout the organization.

In addition to the two cases set out above, in a 2003 report, the Commission on Public Trust and Private Enterprise cited a KPMG survey covering selected US industries; found that 37 percent of employees had, in the previous year, observed misconduct that they believed could result in a significant loss of public trust if it were to become known. This same KPMG survey found that employees reported a variety of types of misconduct and that the employees believed this misconduct is caused most often by factors such as indifference and cynicism; pressure to meet schedules; pressure to hit unrealistic earnings goals; a desire to succeed or advance careers; and a lack of knowledge of standards.

So how can a company overcome these employee attitudes and replace the types of corporate cultures which apparently pervaded at News Corp and re-set its "Tone at the Top"? In a 2008 speech to the State Bar of Texas Annual Meeting, reprinted in Ethisphere, Larry Thompson, PepsiCo Senior Vice President of Governmental Affairs, General Counsel and Secretary, discussed the work of Professor Lynn Sharp at Harvard. From Professor Sharp's writings, Mr. Thompson cited five factors which are critical in establishing an effective integrity program and to set the right "Tone at the Top".

1. The guiding values of a company must make sense and be clearly communicated.
2. The company's leader must be personally committed and willing to take action on the values.

3. A company's systems and structures must support its guiding principles.
4. A company's values must be integrated into normal channels of management decision making and reflected in the company's critical decisions.
5. Managers must be empowered to make ethically sound decisions on a day-to-day basis.

So whether with malicious intent or simply said out of frustration, when Henry II uttered the words which are the title of today's posting, it set the tone for the four knights which overheard him. They set off and murdered Thomas Becket. Perhaps less starkly into today's world, if the tone from the top is that you must meet you quarterly numbers or the company will find someone else to do the job; that is the message that will come across to company employees. But whether you are the King of England, the Chief Executive Officer (CEO) of a Fortune 500 company or simply in a leadership position in your company; the tone does matter.

The FCPA and Tone at the Top and in the Middle

Posted August 8, 2011

Just how important is "Tone at the Top"? Conversely, what does it say to middle management when upper management practices the age old parental line of "Don't do as I act; Do as I say"? We wondered about this age old question as we read the Saturday's edition of the New York Times (NYT) and its piece entitled *"H.P. Ousts Chief for Hiding Payments to Friend"*. In the story, the NYT reported that (now former) Hewlett-Packard (HP) Chairman and Chief Executive (CEO) Mark Hurd was "ousted by the Company's Board of Directors for the lowliest of corporate offenses — fudging his expenses."

The saga apparently began when a contractor who was assisting with HP's marketing contacted the Company in June and through her lawyer charged sexual harassment against Hurd. The NYT reported that while the Board was investigating the sexual harassment charge, they found inaccurate expense reports that covered payments made to the woman. These payments were "said to range from $1,000 to $20,000." After being confronted with the information, Hurd offered to pay back these monies but the Board refused and demanded his resignation, which he tendered. Hurd received $12,224,693 in severance, according to a HP filing with the Securities and Exchange Commission (SEC) on Friday. The Company also "extended the deadline for Hurd to purchase up to 775,000 shares of H.P. common stock, which were vested as of Friday, and 330,117 performance-based stock units that will also vest."

We have previously discussed the importance of "Tone at the Top" and our colleague Lindsay Walker has guest blogged on the subject of "Integrating Ethics and Compliance into the Entire Organization". We both believe that a Company's ethics and compliance culture are set by the very top levels of management. The US government would also appear to believe that a Company's ethics and compliance culture are set by the very top levels of management because the US Sentencing Guidelines read, in part, *"High-level personnel and substantial authority personnel of the organization shall be knowledgeable about the content and operation of the compliance and ethics program ... and shall promote an organizational culture that encourages ethical conduct and a commitment to compliance with the law."*

However if top management is not fully committed to such an ethical and compliance culture, such lack of commitment will be clearly understood by middle managers of a company. This is particularly true of the Foreign Corrupt Practices Act (FCPA). As noted above, the US Sentencing Guidelines mandate that the highest levels of management promote and encourage not only ethical conduct but a commitment to comply with the FCPA itself. In his article, entitled "Ethics and the Middle Manager: Creating "Tone in The Middle"", Kirk Hanson listed eight specific actions that top executives could engage in which demonstrate a company's and their personal commitment to ethics and compliance. The actions he listed were:

> 1. Top executives must themselves exhibit all the "tone at the top" behaviors, including acting ethically, talking frequently about the organization's values and ethics, and supporting the organization's and individual employee's adherence to the values.

2.   Top executives must explicitly ask middle managers what dilemmas arise in implementing the ethical commitments of the organization in the work of that group.

3.   Top executives must give general guidance about how values apply to those specific dilemmas.

4.   Top executives must explicitly delegate resolution of those dilemmas to the middle managers.

5.   Top executives must make it clear to middle managers that their ethical performance is being watched as closely as their financial performance.

6.   Top executives must make ethical competence and commitment of middle managers a part of their performance evaluation.

7.   The organization must provide opportunities for middle managers to work with peers on resolving the hard cases.

8.   Top executives must be available to the middle managers to discuss/coach/resolve the hardest cases.

Given the current situation with the former Chairman and Chief Executive and the ongoing bribery investigation by not only German and Russian governmental authorities but also the SEC and Department of Justice (DOJ) for possible FCPA violations, it might be a propitious time for HP's top management to implement some or all of Hanson's suggestions regarding the communication of HP's commitment to FCPA compliance and ethics to its middle management and, indeed, throughout its organization.

2. Code of Conduct and Compliance Policies and Procedures

<u>Introduction</u>

A company's code of conduct is often the foundation upon which an effective compliance program is built. Additionally, a company should have policies and procedures that outline responsibilities for compliance within the company, detail proper internal controls, auditing practices, and documentation policies, and set forth disciplinary procedures. Among the risks that a company may need to address include the nature and extent of transactions with foreign governments, including payments to foreign officials; use of third parties; gifts, travel, and entertainment expenses; charitable and political donations; and facilitating and expediting payments.

28

A. Code of Conduct

Code of Conduct – The Cornerstone of Your FCPA Compliance Program

Posted February 23, 2011

The cornerstone of a Foreign Corrupt Practices Act (FCPA) compliance program is the US Sentencing Guidelines. They contain seven (7) basic compliance elements that can be tailored to fit the needs and financial realities of any given organization. From these seven compliance elements the Department of Justice (DOJ) has crafted its minimum *best practices* compliance program which is now attached to every Deferred Prosecution Agreement (DPA) and Non-Prosecution Agreement (NPA). The FSG assumes that every effective compliance and ethics program begins with a written standard of conduct; i.e. a Code of Conduct. What should be in this "written standard of conduct? The starting point, as per the US Sentencing Guidelines, reads as follows:

Element 1
Standards of Conduct, Policies and Procedures (a Code of Conduct)
An organization should have an established set of compliance standards and procedures. These standards should not be a "paper only" document, but a living document that promotes organizational culture that encourages "ethical conduct" and a commitment to compliance with applicable regulations and laws.

In each DPA and NPA over the past 18 months the DOJ has said the following as item No. 1 for a minimum *best practices* compliance program.

1. **Code of Conduct. A Company should develop and promulgate a clearly articulated and visible corporate policy against violations of the FCPA, including its anti-bribery, books and records, and internal controls provisions, and other applicable foreign law counterparts (collectively, the "anti-corruption laws"), which policy shall be memorialized in a written compliance code.**

In an article in the Society of Corporate Compliance and Ethics (SCCE) Complete Compliance and Ethics Manual, 2nd Ed., entitled *"Essential Elements of an Effective Ethics and Compliance Program"*, authors Debbie Troklus, Greg Warner and Emma Wollschlager Schwartz, state that your company's Code of Conduct "should demonstrate a complete ethical attitude and your organization's "system-wide" emphasis on compliance and ethics with all applicable laws and regulations." Your Code of Conduct must be aimed at all employees and all representatives of the organization, not just those most actively involved in known compliance and ethics issues. From the board of directors to volunteers, the authors believe that "everyone must receive, read, understand, and agree to abide by the standards of the Code of Conduct." This would also include all "management, vendors, suppliers, and independent contractors, which are frequently overlooked groups."

There are several purposes identified by the authors which should be communicated in your Code of Conduct. Of course the overriding goal is for all employees to follow what is required of them under the Code of Conduct. You can do this in a Code by communicating what is required of them, to provide a process for proper decision-making and then to require that all persons subject to the Code of Conduct put these standards into everyday business practice. Such actions are some of your best evidence that your company "upholds and supports proper compliance conduct."

The substance of your Code of Conduct should be tailored to the company's culture, and to its industry and corporate identity. It should provide a mechanism by which employees who are trying to do the right thing in the compliance and business ethics arena to do so. The Code of Conduct can be used as a basis for employee review and evaluation. It should certainly be invoked if there is a violation. To that end suggest that your company's disciplinary procedures be stated in the Code of Conduct. These would include all forms of disciplines, up to and including dismissal, for serious violations of the Code of Conduct. Further, your company's Code of Conduct should emphasize it will comply with all applicable laws and regulations, wherever it does business. The Code needs to be written in plain English and translated into other languages as necessary so that all applicable persons can understand it.

As I often say, the three most important things about your FCPA compliance program are document, document and then document. The same is true of communicating your company's Code of Conduct. You need to do more than simply put it on your website and tell folks it is there, available and that they should read it. You need to document that all employees, or anyone else that your Code of Conduct is applicable to, has received, read, and understands the Code. For employees, it is important that a representative of the Compliance Department, or other qualified trainer, explains the standards set forth in your Code of Conduct and answers any questions that an employee may have. Your company's employees need to attest in writing that they have received, read, and understood the Code of Conduct and this attestation must be retained and updated as appropriate.

The DOJ expects each company to begin its compliance program with a very public and very robust Code of Conduct. If your company does not have one, you need to implement one forthwith. If your company has not reviewed or assessed your Code of Conduct for five years, I would suggest that you do in short order as much has changed in the compliance world.

Revising Your Code of Conduct - Don't Wait for Another Great Fire of London

Posted September 5, 2012

In 1666 the dates of September 4 and 5 are generally recognized as the worst days of the Great Fire of London. The Great Fire started at the bakery of Thomas Farriner on Pudding Lane, shortly after midnight on Sunday, 2 September, and spread rapidly west across the City of London. The fire gutted the medieval City of London inside the old Roman City Walls. It is estimated to have destroyed the homes of 70,000 of the City's 80,000 inhabitants. The City was rebuilt, with much of the old street plan being recreated in the new City, with improvements in hygiene and fire safety: wider streets, open and accessible wharves along the length of the Thames, with no houses obstructing access to the river, and, most importantly, buildings constructed of brick and stone, not wood. New public buildings were created on their predecessors' sites; the most famous is St. Paul's Cathedral and its smaller cousins, Christopher Wren's 50 new churches.

Not all rebuilding requires such drastic destruction however. In a recent article in the Society of Corporate Compliance and Ethics (SCCE) Magazine, entitled *"Six steps for revising your company's Code of Conduct"*, authors Anne Marie Logarta and Ruth Ward suggest considering the following issues before you take on an update of your Code of Conduct.

- When was the last time your Code of Conduct was released or revised?
- Have there been changes to your company's internal policies since the last revision?

- Have there been changes to relevant laws relating to a topic covered in your company's Code of Conduct?
- Are any of the guidelines outdated?
- Is there a budget to create/revise a Code?

After considering these issues, the authors suggest that you should benchmark your current Code of Conduct against others companies in your industry. If you decide to move forward the authors have a six-point guide which they believe will assist you in making your revision process successful.

1. *Get buy-in from decision makers at the highest level of the company*

The authors believe that your company's highest level must give the mandate for a revision to a Code of Conduct. It should be the Chief Executive Officer (CEO), General Counsel (GC) or Chief Compliance Officer (CCO), or better yet all three to mandate this effort. Whoever gives the mandate, this person should be "consulted at every major step of the Code review process if it involves a change in the direction of key policies."

2. *Establish a core revision committee*

The authors believe that a cross-functional working group should head up your effort to revise your Code of Conduct. They suggest that this group include representatives from the following departments: legal, compliance, communications, HR; there should also be other functions which represent the company's domestic and international business units; finally there should be functions within the company represented such as finance and accounting, IT, marketing and sales.

From this large group, the authors believe that Code of Conduct topics can be assigned for initial drafting to functions based on "relevancy or necessity". These different functions would also solicit feedback from their functional peers and deliver a final, proposed draft to the Drafting Committee. The authors emphasize that creation of a "timeline at the outset of the revision is critical and hold the function representatives accountable for meeting their deliverables."

3. Conduct a thorough technology assessment

The authors argue that the backbone of the revision process is how your company captures, collaborates and preserves "all of the comments, notes, edits and decisions during the entire project." They believe that technology such as SharePoint or Google Cloud can be of great assistance to accomplish this process even if you are required to train team members on their use.

In addition to this use of technology in drafting your Code of Conduct revision, you should determine if your Code of Conduct will be available in hard copy, online or both. If it will be available online, you should assess "the best application to launch your Code and whether it includes a certification process". Lastly, there must be a distribution plan, particularly if the Code will only be available in hard copy.

4. Determine translations and localizations

The authors emphasize that "If your company does business internationally, then this step is vital to ensure you have one Code, no matter the language." They do note that if you decide to translate your Code of Conduct be sure and hire someone who is an "approved company translation subject matter expert." Here I would simply say to contact Jay Rosen at Merrill Brink, as those guys are the SMEs and know what they are doing when it comes to translations. The key is that "your employees have the same understanding of the company's Code-no matter the language."

5. *Develop a plan to communicate the Code of Conduct*

A roll-out is always critical because it "is important that the new or revised Code is communicated in a manner that encourages employees to review and use the Code on an ongoing basis." The authors believe that your company should use the full panoply of tools available to it to publicize your new or revised Code of Conduct. This can include a multi-media approach or physically handing out a copy to all employees at a designated time. You might consider having a company-wide Code of Conduct meeting where the new or revised Code is rolled out across the company all in one day. But remember, with all thing compliance; the three most important aspects are Document, Document and Document. However you deliver the new or revised Code of Conduct, you must document that each employee receives it.

6. *Stay on Target*

The authors end by noting that if you set realistic expectations you should be able to stay on deadline and stay within your budget. They state that "You want to set aside enough time so that you won't feel rushed or in a hurry to get it done." They also reiterate to keep a close watch on your budget so that you do not exceed it.

Logarta and Ward's article provides a useful guide to not only thinking through how to determine if your Code of Conduct needs updating, but also practical steps on how to tackle the problem. If you are a compliance practitioner, I would urge you to take a look at your company's Code of Conduct. If it has been more than five years since it was last updated, you should begin the process that the authors have laid out. Do not wait for a catastrophe like the City of London did with the Great Fire of London to rebuild. It is far better to review and update if appropriate than wait for a massive Foreign Corrupt Practices Act (FCPA) investigation to go through the process.

B. Gifts, Travel and Business Entertainment

How Casanova Informs Your FCPA Compliance Program

Posted October 15, 2012

An article in the New York Times (NYT) entitled *"Strauss-Kahn Say Sex Parties Went Too Far, But Lust Is No Crime"* caught my eye. In the article reporters Doreen Carvajal and Maia de la Baume detailed the libertine sex life of the former Managing Director of the International Monetary Fund (IMF) Dominique Strauss-Kahn (DSK).

1.   *The Times Article*

It turns out that DSK's little tryst with the maid in the hotel in New York was but a small sampling of his escapades. According to the NYT article, "The exclusive orgies called "parties fines" — lavish Champagne affairs costing around $13,000 each — were organized as a roving international circuit from Paris to Washington by businessmen seeking to ingratiate themselves with Mr. Strauss-Kahn. Some of that money, according to a lawyer for the main host, ultimately paid for prostitutes because of a shortage of women at the mixed soirees orchestrated largely for the benefit of Mr. Strauss-Kahn, who sometimes sought sex with three or four women." Apparently such events had a long and treasured history in France where "Libertinage" goes back to the 16th Century.

According to DSK he said, "I long thought that I could lead my life as I wanted," in an interview with the French magazine Le Point. "And that includes free behavior between consenting adults." Ah those French. Where is Casanova when you need him to explain how a Frenchman needs a little *liaison* with 3 or 4 women now and again?

However, it turns out that our Libertine DSK was not exactly paying for 'services rendered'. These sex romps cost a lot of money, as stated in the NYT article, over $13,000 per event. The events started out with lavish dinners and then couples would pair off and pair off and pair off. (Cue the Viagra pop-up ad now.) More ominously, DSK did not pay for these events himself. The NYT article quoted Karl Vandamme, a defense lawyer who represents Fabrice Paszkowski, the owner of a medical supply company who played a crucial role in organizing the sex parties. "Libertines are people like you and me: people who have a normal life," said Mr. Vandamme, who said his client invested around $65,000 in party expenses, *betting on the political rise of Mr. Strauss-Kahn*." (Emphasis mine)

So what is the Foreign Corrupt Practices Act (FCPA) compliance angle here? I think that everyone would agree that providing prostitutes to foreign governmental officials to obtain or retain business would be a violation of the FCPA. But here there are a couple of points that I found of interest far beyond simply providing hookers.

2. *FCPA Application*

a. Covered Recipient

The first is who precisely does the FCPA cover? Certainly it covers foreign governmental officials and I would certainly argue that it covers employees of state owned enterprises and it does cover other persons as well. Under the FCPA officers or employees of public international organizations are covered. The definition reads as follows:

For purposes of this section:

(1) A) The term "foreign official" means any officer or employee of a foreign government or any department, agency, or instrumentality thereof, or *of a public international organization*, or any person acting in an official capacity for or on behalf of any such government or department, agency, or instrumentality, or *for or on behalf of any such public international organization.* (emphasis supplied)

The IMF is a public international organization. Prior to becoming the Managing Director (MD) of the IMF in 2007, DSK was active in French politics, holding several government offices and even unsuccessfully running for the Socialist Party candidate for President in 2007. He was the MD of the IMF from 2007 until he resigned after having been accused of sexual assault by a hotel maid in New York City in 2012.

b. Obtain or Retain Business

So our Libertine friend DSK could be covered by the FCPA if a US company was participating in conduct which would violate the FCPA. One person was quoted in the NYT article that his client, both personally and through his company, invested money to pay for the sex romps "betting on the political rise" of DSK. The FCPA makes illegal "use of the mails or any means or instrumentality of interstate commerce corruptly in furtherance of an offer, payment, promise to pay, or authorization of the payment of any money, or offer, gift, promise to give, or authorization of the giving of anything of value" which are intended to do any of the following:

(A)(i) influencing any act or decision of such foreign official in his official capacity, (ii) inducing such foreign official to do or omit to do any act in violation of the lawful duty of such official, or (iii) securing any improper advantage; or

(B) inducing such foreign official to use his influence with a foreign government or instrumentality thereof to affect or influence any act or decision of such government or instrumentality, in order to assist such issuer in obtaining or retaining business for or with, or directing business to, any person

Here we have clients paying for lavish gift parties, which I would argue are *per se* unreasonable under the Gifts and Entertain affirmative defense under the FCPA. (No snickers here please as I am not arguing that a $100 for hooker is reasonable.) Further, the clear intent of at least the client of the above quoted Mr. Vandamme was "betting on the political rise of" DSK. Think the client, Fabrice Paszkowski, the owner of a medical supply company, was just shelling out that kind of money so DSK could 'enjoy himself' or is it more probable that Paszkowski, would expect to "obtain or retain" some business or other benefit from his now sated buddy DSK?

There are several learning moments from the fall of DSK and FCPA compliance. The first is to remember that the FCPA covers more than simply foreign government officials and employees of state owned enterprises. As stated it also covers officers and employees of public international organizations. It is even broader as it also covers political parties and those seeking political office in foreign countries. The DSK Libertine Sex Party lifestyle also reminds us that the FCPA not only prohibits bribes paid in cash but the ubiquitous "anything of value". (And no I am not going to debate whether having sex with four partners a night is "anything of value" particularly if Viagra is included in the cost.)

It could certainly be interesting if the names of any companies subject to the FCPA come up in the ongoing investigation into DSK.

The Wolfman and Opinion Release 12-02

Posted October 31, 2012

> *Even a man who is pure in heart,*
> *and says his prayers by night,*
> *may become a wolf when the wolfsbane blooms,*
> *and the autumn moon is bright.*

Today is Halloween and in this post I conclude my celebration of the Universal Pictures classic monster movies from the 30s and 40s. Today I submit, for your compliance consideration, my favorite of the classic monsters movies *The Wolfman*. I simply cannot see this movie enough. From the horrific scene where Lon Chaney Jr. kills Bela, the gypsy who had the pentagram, the mark of the wolf, to the ending scene where Claude Rains inadvertently kills his son, Lon Chaney Jr., in his incarnation as the beast with a silver tipped cane, I find it to be the most psychologically complex of all the classic Universal monsters.

The acting was first rate. Lon Chaney Jr. as Larry brought a psychologically-nuance to the role that rivals only Karloff as Frankenstein's Monster for depth and complexity. Claude Rains, although a good 6 inches shorter than Chaney, plays his father Sir John Talbot and showed why he was one of the great character actors from the 1930s to the 1960s. Maria Ouspenskaya as the gypsy fortuneteller Maleva who cares for Chaney after he has been attacked by her son and changed into a werewolf brings heart and soul to a role which could have easily fallen into camp. And then there is Evelyn Ankers as Gwen Conliffe, Talbot's love interest. In many ways she ascended to the 'damsel in distress' role created by Fay Wray in King Kong. She is gorgeous in the role and just the right amount of innocence and sex appeal.

In the twilight and with low hanging shrouds of fog, Larry attempts to rescue Gwen's friend Jenny from what he believes to be a sudden wolf attack, he kills the beast with his new walking stick, but is bitten on the chest in the process. The gypsy fortune teller, Maleva, reveals to Larry that the animal which bit him was actually her son Bela (played by the omnipresent Béla Lugosi) in the form of a wolf. She tells Larry that Bela had been a werewolf for years and now he would be transformed into one. When the full moon rises, the sign of the Pentagram appears on Larry and he is transformed into a wolf-like creature and stalks the village, first killing the local gravedigger. He retains vague memories of being a werewolf and wanting to kill, and continually struggles to overcome his condition. He is finally bludgeoned to death by Sir John, with his own silver walking stick, after attacking Gwen.

My favorite scene? It actually occurs in the first sequel, *Frankenstein Meets The Wolfman*, where two forlorn grave robbers break into the Talbot Family Crypt, where Larry is buried after being killed by his father at the end of the original *Wolfman* movie. They pry open the burial tomb just as the full moon is arising, which of course awakens the beast in Larry. He transforms into the Wolfman and kills the grave robbers. It simply is a fantastic cacophony of light, shading, violence, folklore and terror.

So what does *The Wolfman* introduce from the compliance perspective? In this case, it is reverse psychology. It is the latest Department of Justice (DOJ) Opinion Release, 12-02, which was dated October 18, 2012 but was not released publicly until last week. In 12-02 certain Requestors, which were 19 non-profit adoption agencies located in the US, asked the DOJ about bringing certain foreign governmental officials involved in the foreign country's adoption process to the US. All the foreign governmental officials are involved in the process of allowing children from their country go through the adoption process with the US non-profits involved. The trips to the US will be for two days of meetings.

The purpose of the visit will be to demonstrate the Requestors' work to the government officials so that the officials can see how adopted children from the foreign country have adjusted to life in the US and to help the Requestors learn how they can ensure that they provide the foreign country's government with appropriate information during the adoption process. The Requestors will allow the government officials to meet with the Requestors' employees and to inspect the Requestors' offices and case files from previous adoptions. The foreign country's government officials will also meet with families who have adopted children from their country and learn more about the Requestors' work.

In this Opinion Release, the DOJ opined on a question regarding the payment for travel of these foreign governmental officials and whether the proposed trip would violate the Foreign Corrupt Practices Act (FCPA).

The Opinion Release set out the representations made by the Requestors to the DOJ which formed the basis for its decision. The Requestors stated that they would pay for the following:

- Business class airfare on international portions of flights for ministers, members of the legislature, and the director of the Orphanage Agency; coach airfare for international portions of flights for all other government officials; and coach airfare for domestic portions of flights for all government officials;

- Two or three nights hotel stay at a business-class hotel;
- Meals during the officials' stays; and
- Transportation between agencies and local transportation.

The DOJ also noted the Requestors spending on meals and hotels would not exceed the rate set by the US General Services Administration for US government employees traveling within the US. The Requestors also made the following presentations which are consistent with prior DOJ guidance on travel, meals and entertainment.

- **Entertainment** - The entertainment will be of nominal cost and will involve families who have adopted children from the foreign country. In other words, a clear business purpose is involved.
- **Selection** - The Requestors did not select the foreign governmental officials to attend the trip but left that decision to the foreign government.
- **No WAGS** - The Requestors would only host the foreign governmental officials selected for the trip. There would be no spouses or family members brought along on this trip.
- **Souvenirs** - If there are any souvenirs presented to the visiting foreign officials, they will be of nominal value.
- **Spending money** - There will be no spending money provided to the foreign officials and they will not receive any stipends. There will be no additional monies paid to the visiting officials in any form.

So while poor Larry Talbot was doomed to run afoul of the laws of man when he became the Wolfman, you need not have the same result under your compliance program. I believe that Opinion Release 12-02 shows once again that if you have a compliance question or concern, the Opinion Release procedure is available to you to ask the DOJ if your proposed activity would violate the FCPA. But more than simply showing the procedure, I think that the DOJ once again shows how a reasoned approach, laid out in a rational manner, will be seriously considered, reviewed and can lead to a favorable result. Even the question of business class airfare can be handled in reasoned approach as shown by this Opinion Release. I disagree with the FCPA Professor in that there is a "high level of anxiety and skittishness in this current era of FCPA enforcement out there" because, as this Opinion Release shows, you need not fear FCPA enforcement, even *when the wolfsbane blooms, and the autumn moon is bright.*

C. Charitable Donations

Opinion Release 10-02 and Charitable Donations under the FCPA

Posted July 25, 2010

What is a company to do if, in order to obtain a contract with a foreign government, they must agree to invest a percentage of the proceeds of the transaction into the community in which it operates as a "charitable donation"? This is negotiated with the foreign government and can include cash or in-kind contributions of computers, equipment or appliances to schools, communities or organizations.

While not a payment to a governmental official, it is still a payment to a governmental entity for the purpose of securing a lucrative contract and requires careful consideration. This spectra is currently required in some countries by law and these payments have generated some questions with regard to compliance with the Foreign Corrupt Practices Act (FCPA) as such donations could be interpreted as corruptly giving or offering anything of value to any "foreign official" in order to assist "in obtaining or retaining business for or with, or directing any business to, any person . . . ." 15 U.S.C. § 78dd-2(a)(1).

This past week the Department of Justice (DOJ) published its second FCPA Opinion Procedure Release of 2010, 10-02. The release dealt with a US based micro financial institution (MFI) operating in an unnamed Eurasian country. This MFI desired to convert its local operations from a "humanitarian status" to a commercial status. The relevant government licensing authority in the country in question required that as a condition precedent to obtaining this commercial license, the MFI would be required to make a substantial grant to some other local MFIs, providing a list of one or more that the US MFI could choose. The US MFI was concerned that by making such a donation a condition precedent and specifying the list of local MFIs to which the donation could be made, the US MFI could run afoul of the FCPA's proscription of "corruptly giving or offering anything of value to any foreign official" in order to assist "in obtaining or retaining business for or with, or directing any business to, any person . . . ."

In stating that the DOJ "does not intend to take any enforcement action with regard to the proposed transaction" the Opinion Release specified the three levels of due diligence that the US MFI had engaged in on the proposed locals MFIs which were listed as eligible to receive the funding. The DOJ noted that [it] "is satisfied, however, that the Requestor has done appropriate due diligence and that the controls that it plans to institute are sufficient to prevent FCPA violations. As noted above, the Requestor [US MFI] conducted three rounds of due diligence. The controls that the Requestor proposes would ensure with reasonable certainty that the grant money from the Eurasian Subsidiary would not be transferred to officials of the Eurasian country."

In addition to the specific discussion of the due diligence performed by the US MFI and noting the controls it had put in place after the funding was scheduled to be made the DOJ also listed several of the due diligence and/or controls that it had previously set forth in prior Opinion Releases relating to charitable donations. These included:

- certifications by the recipient that it will comply with the requirements of the FCPA;

- due diligence to confirm that none of the recipient's officers or directors are affiliated with the foreign government at issue;
- a requirement that the recipient provide audited financial statements;
- a written agreement with the recipient restricting the use of funds to humanitarian or charitable purposes only;
- steps to ensure that the funds were transferred to a valid bank account;
- confirmation that contemplated activities had occurred before funds were disbursed; and
- ongoing auditing and monitoring of the efficacy of the program.

Opinion Release 10-02 provides a wealth of information to the FCPA practitioner and compliance counsel. It gives specific guidance on the levels of due diligence that a US company should go through when investigating a charitable institution selected, or suggested by a foreign governmental official, to be the recipient of a company's charitable donations. Further, it lists the controls that a US company can and should put in place, should it determine that a charitable donation is to be made. In short Opinion Release 10-02 gives significant guidance in pre-donation due diligence investigation, evaluation and post donation monitoring going forward to manage the process. Opinion Release 10-02 is a very large and helpful educational tool in the FCPA compliance arena. We welcome its release.

Compelled Giving and the FCPA

Posted July 30, 2010

The recent post on charitable donations under the Foreign Corrupt Practices Act (FCPA) and Opinion Release 10-02 brought an interesting dialogue with fellow blogger, the FCPA Professor. The FCPA Professor raised the issue of *"compelled giving"* disguised as a requirement that a US company doing business overseas makes a charitable donation with the implicit understanding that such a requirement is mandated to obtain or retain business by a foreign governmental official and how such payments would be viewed under the FCPA. We believe that the underlying facts of the Opinion Release referenced demonstrate that the Department of Justice (DOJ) has recognized that *compelled giving* is a situation that is faced by US companies doing business overseas, if not on a regular basis, but certainly one that is not unknown.

In Venezuela energy service contracts with the national oil company, PDVSA requires that the foreign company must agree to invest an established percentage of the profits from each contract into the community in which it operates. This is negotiated with the Venezuelan government and can include cash or in-kind contributions of computers, equipment or appliances to schools, communities or organizations. This requirement may also be present in contracts for infrastructure opportunities including communications and transportation.

Although it is legal and a practice required by law in Venezuela, these payments have generated some questions with regards to compliance with the FCPA and similar laws of other countries. While not a payment to a governmental official, it is still a payment to a governmental entity for the purpose of securing a contract. It may also be that a governmental official sits on the Board of the local charity in question. Such issues require careful consideration.

There appears to be only one FCPA enforcement action based entirely upon charitable giving. It is the case of Schering-Plough Poland which paid a $500,000 civil penalty assessed by the Securities and Exchange Commission (SEC) in 2008. As reported in the FCPA Blog, the Company's Polish subsidiary made improper payments to a charitable organization named the Chudow Castle Foundation, which was headed by an individual who was the Director of the Silesian Health Fund during the time period in question. Schering-Plough is a pharmaceutical company and the Director of the Health Fund provided money for the purchase of products manufactured by Schering-Plough as well as influencing medical institutions, such as hospitals, in their purchase of pharmaceutical products through the allocation of health fund resources. In addition to the above, the SEC found that Schering-Plough did not accurately record these charitable donations on the company's books and records.

The FCPA Blog further reported that when asked about the guidelines regarding requests for charitable giving and the FCPA the then Deputy Chief of the Criminal Division's Fraud Section at the DOJ Mark Mendelsohn, said that any such request must be evaluated on its own merits. He advocated a "common sense" approach in identifying and clearing *Red Flags.* This would include determining if a governmental decision maker held a position of authority at the charity to which the donation would be made, whether the donation was consistent with a company's overall pattern of charitable giving, who made the request for the donation and how was it made.

The series of **Red Flags** raised and cleared by the US Company which was the subject of Opinion Release 10-02. After initially listing the 3 levels of due diligence in which the company had engaged prior to finalizing its choice of local entity to receive the donation in question; the DOJ noted that the donation 'requested' of the US Company would be subject to the following controls:

1. Payments of the donations would be staggered over a period of eight quarters rather than in one lump sum.
2. Ongoing monitoring and auditing of the funds use for a period of five years.
3. The donations would be specifically utilized for the building of infrastructure.
4. The funds would not be paid to the parent of the organization receiving the grant and there was an absolute prohibition on compensating Board Members.
5. The proposed grant agreement under which the funds would be donated had significant anti-corruption provisions which included a requirement that the local organization receiving the funds adopt an anti-corruption policy and that US Company making the donation receive full access to the local organization's books and records.

Both the underlying due diligence and the controls noted above led the DOJ to state "The Department is satisfied, however, that the Requestor has done appropriate due diligence and that the controls that it plans to institute are sufficient to prevent FCPA violations."

In addition to the specific factors presented by the requesting US company in Opinion Release 10-02, the DOJ also listed several of the due diligence and/or controls that it had previously set forth in prior Opinion Releases relating to charitable donations. These included:

- certifications by the recipient that it will comply with the requirements of the FCPA;
- due diligence to confirm that none of the recipient's officers or directors are affiliated with the foreign government at issue;
- a requirement that the recipient provide audited financial statements;
- a written agreement with the recipient restricting the use of funds to humanitarian or charitable purposes only;
- steps to ensure that the funds were transferred to a valid bank account;
- confirmation that contemplated activities had occurred before funds were disbursed; and
- ongoing auditing and monitoring of the efficacy of the program.

We believe that Opinion Release 10-02 addresses some of the concerns of US companies in the area of *compelled giving*; particularly in view of the enforcement action involving Schering-Plough. The DOJ, once again, has indicated that extensive due diligence, coupled with the best practices in compliance management going forward after the contract is executed, appear to be critical in its analysis.

D. Facilitation Payments

Does Wal-Mart Have a Facilitation Payment Exception to the FCPA?

Posted April 25, 2012

In an article entitled *"Many Of The Bribery Allegations Against Wal-Mart May Not Be Illegal"* Forbes reporter Nathan Vardi wrote that "many of the allegations reported in the New York Times could reasonably be interpreted as falling under the so-called "facilitating payments" exception." I wondered what defense might be available to Wal-Mart where bribes of up to $244,000 could be construed as an exception to prosecution for bribery of foreign government official under the Foreign Corrupt Practices Act (FCPA). In this post we will visit the text of the FCPA and other Department of Justice (DOJ) commentary, look at some enforcement actions; one open investigation involving alleged facilitation payments and offer some guidance to the compliance practitioner on what may or may not constitute a facilitation payment under the FCPA.

I. *The Statute and Other Guidance*

A. The Statute

Interestingly, when the FCPA was initially passed in 1977, the facilitating payment exception was found under the definition of foreign official. However, with the 1988 Amendments, a more explicit exception was written into the statute making it clear that the anti-bribery provisions "shall not apply to any facilitating or expediting payment to a foreign official, political party, or party official the purpose of which is to expedite or to secure the performance of a routine governmental action . . ." The statute itself provided a list of examples of facilitation payments in the definition of routine governmental actions. It included the following:

- Obtaining permits, licenses, or other official documents;
- Processing governmental papers such as visas and work orders;
- Providing police protection, mail services, scheduling inspections;
- Providing utilities, cargo handling; or
- Actions of a similar nature.

It is important to note that the language of the FCPA makes it clear that a facilitation payment is not an affirmative defense but an exception to the general FCPA proscription against bribery and corruption. Unfortunately for the FCPA Practitioner there is no dollar limit articulated in the FCPA regarding facilitation payments. Even this limited exception has come under increasing criticism. The Organization for Economic Cooperation and Development (OECD) studied the issue and, in November 2009, recommended that member countries encourage their corporations to not allow the making of facilitating payments.

B. Lay Person's Guide to the FCPA

The Lay Person's Guide to the FCPA is a brochure by the DOJ which is their "general explanation of the FCPA." Within in this guidance the DOJ states:

FACILITATING PAYMENTS FOR ROUTINE GOVERNMENTAL ACTIONS

There is an exception to the anti-bribery prohibition for payments to facilitate or expedite performance of a "routine governmental action." The statute lists the following examples: obtaining permits, licenses, or other official documents; processing governmental papers, such as visas and work orders; providing police protection, mail pick-up and delivery; providing phone service, power and water supply, loading and unloading cargo, or protecting perishable products; and scheduling inspections associated with contract performance or transit of goods across country.

Actions "similar" to these are also covered by this exception. If you have a question about whether a payment falls within the exception, you should consult with counsel. You should also consider whether to utilize the Justice Department's Foreign Corrupt Practices Opinion Procedure, described in the guide on p. 10 and below:

"Routine governmental action" does not include any decision by a foreign official to award new business or to continue business with a particular party.

II.   *Enforcement Actions*

A. Con-way

The FCPA landscape is littered with companies who sustained FCPA violations due to payments which did not fall into the facilitation payment exception. In 2008, Con-way, a global freight forwarder, paid a $300,000 penalty for making hundreds of relatively small payments to Customs Officials in the Philippines. The value of the payments Con-way was fined for making totaled $244,000 and were made to induce the officials to violate customs regulations, settle customs disputes, and reduce or not enforce otherwise legitimate fines for administrative violations.

B. Helmerich and Payne

In 2009, Helmerich and Payne paid a penalty and disgorgement fee of $1.3 million for payments which were made to secure customs clearances in Argentina and Venezuela. The payments ranged from $2,000 to $5,000 but were not properly recorded and were made to import/export goods that were not within the respective country's regulations; to import goods that could not lawfully be imported; and to evade higher duties and taxes on the goods.

C. Panalpina

Finally, there is the Panalpina enforcement action. As reported in the FCPA Blog, this matter was partly resolved last year with the payment by Panalpina and six of its customers of over $257 million in fines and penalties. Panalpina, acting as freight forwarder for its customers, made payments to circumvent import laws, reduce customs duties and tax assessments and to obtain preferential treatment for importing certain equipment into various countries but primarily in West Africa.

D. DynCorp

Then there is the DynCorp investigation matter. As reported in the FCPA Blog and others, it is related to some $300,000 in payments made by subcontractors who wished to speed up their visa processing and expedite receipt of certain licenses on behalf of DynCorp. This investigation has been going on for several years and there is no anticipated conclusion date at this time.

III.   *Some Guidance*

So what does the DOJ look at when it reviews a company's FCPA compliance program with regards to facilitation payments? Initially, if there is a pattern of such small payments, it would raise a Red Flag and cause additional investigation, but this would not be the end of the inquiry. There are several other factors which the DOJ could look towards in making a final determination on this issue. The line of inquiry the DOJ would take is as follows:

1. **Size of payment** - Is there an outer limit? No, there is no outer limit but there is some line where the perception shifts. If a facilitating payment is over $100 you are arguing from a point of weakness. The presumption of good faith is against you. You might be able to persuade the government at an amount under $100. But anything over this amount and the government may well make further inquiries. So, for instance, the DOJ might say that all facilitation payments should be accumulated together and this would be a pattern and practice of bribery.

2. **What is a routine governmental action?** Are we entitled to this action, have we met all of our actions or are we asking the government official to look the other way on some requirement? Are we asking the government official to give us a break? The key question here is whether you are entitled to the action otherwise.

3. **Does the seniority of the governmental official matter**? This is significant because it changes the presumption of whether something is truly discretionary. The higher the level of the

governmental official involved, the greater chance his decision is discretionary.

4. **Does the action have to be non-discretionary?** Yes, because if it is discretionary, then a payment made will appear to obtaining some advantage that is not available to others.

5. **What approvals should be required?** A facilitation payment is something that must be done with an appropriate process. The process should have thought and the decision made by people who are the experts within the company on such matters.

6. **Risk of facilitation payments and third parties?** Whatever policy you have, it must be carried over to third parties acting on your behalf or at your direction. If a third party cannot control this issue, the better compliance practice would be to end the business relationship.

7. **How should facilitation payments be recorded?** Facilitation payments must be recorded accurately. You should have a category entitled "Facilitation Payments" in your company's internal accounting system. The labeling should be quite clear and they are critical to any audit trail so recording them is quite significant.

8. **Monitoring programs?** There must always be ongoing monitoring programs to review your company's internal controls, policies and procedures regarding facilitation payments.

So we return to the question of when does a grease payment become a bribe? There is no clear line of demarcation. The test seems to turn on the amount of money involved, to whom it is paid and the frequency of the payments. Do Wal-Mart's alleged payments to speed up the process qualify as facilitation payments or does an aggregate of over $24 million paid constitute something else?

Additionally, accurate books and records are a must. At this point it is not apparent if Wal-Mart accurately recorded these payments. If Wal-Mart really believed they were facilitation payments, why didn't they just record them as such?

Also remember that the defense of facilitation payments is an exception to the FCPA prohibition against bribery. Any defendant which wishes to avail itself of this exception at trial would have to proffer credible evidence to support its position, but at the end of the day, it would be the trier of fact which would decide. So much like any compliance defense, the exception is only available if you use it at trial and it would be difficult to imagine that Wal-Mart will want this matter to ever see the light of a courtroom.

Days of Future Passed: The Moody Blues and the End of Facilitation Payments?

Posted December 17, 2012

> *Nights in White Satin, never reaching the end,*
> *Letters I've Written, never meaning to send*

This past weekend I caught the Moody Blues' tour celebrating the 45th anniversary of their seminal classic album, *"Days of Future Passed"*. This was the second album released by the band and while I had always thought of it as the first rock concept album, it is seen by many rock critics as a precursor to progressive rock music. Bill Holdship, Yahoo! Music, said that the band "created an entire genre here." Robert Christgau noted that it was "closer to high-art pomp than psychedelia." And finally, Allmusic editor Bruce Eder calls the album "one of the defining documents of the blossoming psychedelic era, and one of the most enduringly popular albums of its era." The band had its core members of Justin Hayward, John Lodge and Graeme Edge playing at the concert and I can assure you that even in their 70s, they can still rock.

I thought about this album and its title while reading the Memorandum and Order from District Judge Keith Ellison in the Security and Exchange Commission (SEC) civil action filed against current and former officers of Noble Corporation, Mark A. Jackson and James R. Ruehlen. The Foreign Corrupt Practices Act (FCPA) commentariat has gone both ways on interpreting the Court's Order; witness the headline by the FCPA Professor, *"Judge Grants Jackson And Ruehlen's Motion To Dismiss SEC's Monetary Claims – Finds That SEC Was Not Diligent In Bringing Case And That SEC Failed To Negate Facilitation*

Payments Exception – However Judge Allows SEC To File An Amended Complaint", in contrast with Dick Cassin on the FCPA Blog, whose headline read "*Great guidance from the bench: The FCPA casts a wide net*". However, I found one other part of the Court's ruling by far the most interesting. It was the section which discussed whether the defendant's claims that their actions met the facilitation payment exception under the FCPA. The Court granted the SEC leave to amend to proffer facts which would overcome the facilitation payment exception.

The allegations of facilitation payment exception as a defense in this lawsuit turn on permits called Temporary Import Permits (TIPs) in Nigeria. As set out in the Court's ruling, "TIPs allow drilling rigs to operate in Nigerian waters without payment of permanent import duties. Under Nigerian law, the Nigeria Customs Service ("NCS") grants TIPs for rigs that will be in the country for only one year. NCS may, in its discretion, grant up to three six-month extensions to a TIP. Upon the expiration of a TIP and any TIP extensions, NCS requires the rig to be exported from Nigeria. If the owner of the rig wishes to continue using the rig after the expiration of a TIP and any applicable extensions, he can either convert the rig to permanent import status and pay the appropriate permanent import duties, or he can export the rig and seek a new rig TIP to re-import the rig. In order to obtain a TIP or an extension, the rig owner must submit an application thought a licensed customs agent as the NCS does not deal directly with rig owners such as Noble. The SEC alleged that the defendants authorized customer agents to submit false paperwork and pay bribes to NCS officials to obtain these TIPs. In other words, the SEC alleged that the Nobel officials knew that the company was not entitled to obtain the TIPs as they did not meet the basic requirements for the granting of such licenses."

Judge Ellison, in his ruling, noted that the "SEC alleges that Defendants authorized payments to foreign officials in order to obtain TIPs based on false paperwork, in contravention of what Defendants knew was the proper process for obtaining TIPs. As discussed supra in Part III.A.1, the SEC pled sufficient facts to support the allegation that Defendants knew these payments would be going to Nigerian government officials to obtain TIPs in a manner that violated Nigerian law. The grant of permits by government officials that have no authority to grant permits on the basis sought is in no way a ministerial act nor can it be characterized as "speeding the proper performance of a foreign official's duties." Similarly, if payments were made to induce officials to validate the paperwork while knowing it to be false, that too would not qualify as simply expediting a ministerial act." [all citations by Court omitted]

The FCPA states that it "shall not apply to any facilitating or expediting payment to a foreign official, political party, or party official the purpose of which is to expedite or to secure the performance of a routine governmental action . . ." Further, the FCPA has a list of examples of facilitation payments in the definition of routine governmental actions, which include the following:

- Obtaining permits, licenses, or other official documents;
- Processing governmental papers such as visas and work orders;
- Providing police protection, mail services, scheduling inspections;
- Providing utilities, cargo handling; or
- Actions of a similar nature.

The key has always been whether the function in question was a "routine governmental action" because a facilitation payment is clearly a bribe. From the Court's discussion, it is clear that it is thinking that if the end goal of a facilitation payment is to obtain something that the person or entity making the facilitation knows that they are not entitled to, then it cannot be a facilitation payment because it is not a "routine governmental action". However, the Court also focused on "corruptly" and cited to the legislative history of the statute for the following:

> *The word "corruptly" is used in order to make clear that the offer, payment, promise, or gift, must be intended to induce the recipient to misuse his official position; for example, . . . to induce a foreign official to fail to perform an official function. The word "corruptly" connotes an evil motive or purpose such as that required under 18 U.S.C. 201(b) which prohibits domestic bribery. As in 18 U.S.C. 201(b), the word "corruptly" indicates an intent or desire to wrongfully influence the recipient.*

As part of its instructions to the SEC to re-plead the Court said that it should plead Nigerian law to show this corrupt intent. If the SEC does this and the illegal nature of the defendants' actions under Nigerian law forms a basis of a successful action, how long do you think it will be before the entire concept of the facilitation payment comes in an enforcement action as there is no country in the world which allows bribery of its own government officials?

If the Court continues down this path, we may see the United States move towards a de facto end of the facilitation payment exception. The OECD, among others, has urged the United States to ban these types of bribes.

The UK Bribery Act has no such exception under it. Numerous commentators, including Jon Jordan, have argued eloquently for the facilitation payment exception to end.

So what about the Moody Blues and *Days of Future Passed*? Just as many people remember only the song "*Nights In White Satin*" from the album and do not recall its greater importance as the either the first concept album or as a precursor to progressive rock, analysts and commentators may miss the significance of Judge Ellison's ruling as it may signal the first step on the judicial journey to end facilitation payments.

E. Internal Controls

Internal Controls under the FCPA

Posted January 31, 2011

Most Foreign Corrupt Practices Act (FCPA) practitioners understand the requirement for a compliance policy under the FCPA. However many practitioners, particularly lawyers practicing in the compliance field, do not understand the requirement for proper Internal Controls. Generally speaking, Internal Controls are policies, procedures and training which are installed to safeguard that a business' assets are utilized in an appropriate manner; with proper oversight and approval and that all company transactions are properly recorded in its books and records.

We have previously discussed the new book by Aaron Murphy in the FCPA arena, entitled *"Foreign Corrupt Practices Act – A Practical Resource for Managers and Executives"*. In this work, Mr. Murphy opines that Internal Controls can be delineated into five concepts, which are as follows:

I.   **Risk Assessment** - A company should assess the compliance risks associated with its business.
II. **Corporate Compliance Policy and Code of Conduct** - A company should have an overall governance document which will inform employees throughout the company, of the conduct the company expects from an employee. If the company is global/multi-national, this document should be translated into the relevant languages as appropriate.
III. **Implementing Procedures** - A company should have a written set of procedures in place that

instructs employees on the details of how to comply with the company's compliance policy.

IV. **Training** - A company should have a training program in place to confirm that employees understand their obligations under the compliance policies and procedures.

V. **Monitor Compliance** - A company must test, assess and audit to determine if its compliance policies and procedures are a 'living and breathing program' and not just a paper tiger.

While all of the above may seem to be covered by the US Sentencing Guidelines, as the *best practices* of any robust compliance program, the lack of Internal Controls can bring serious consequences to any company found violating the FCPA. The failure to maintain proper Internal Controls can bring a separate civil charge, brought by the Securities and Exchange Commission (SEC). Such a charge can lead to a fine, injunction and profit disgorgement.

With the above in mind, we would propose, as a starting point for the FCPA practitioner, our own five questions to start the assessment of your company's Internal Controls. They are:

1. What accounting processes, if any, occur outside your home office and at how many locations?

2. What ERP/financial accounting software system is used? Is the same system used at each location where accounting is performed?

3. Who are the independent auditors and for how many years have they been performing audits for the Company?

4. Has there ever been an independent assessment of Internal Controls, other than what is done in connection with the independent audit?
5. Has there ever been fraud detected in the Company?

While Internal Controls is often seen as the step-child in any FCPA compliance discussion, we believe that Internal Controls should be seen as a bulwark in a *best practices* compliance program to prevent, detect and help remedy any situation which may be violative of the FCPA. We would also note that robust Internal Controls is also considered to be a key component of any *adequate procedures* under the UK Bribery Act. We hope that the five questions we have listed above may be a good starting point for you to begin to assess your company's Internal Controls.

FCPA Lessons Learned - Failures in Internal Controls

Posted March 28, 2011

We often write and speak on some of the lesson learned from enforcement actions brought by the Department of Justice (DOJ) under the Foreign Corrupt Practices Act (FCPA). We believe that companies can not only learn from the mistakes of others in implementing or enhancing their compliance program but can glean information on the DOJ's current thinking on the *best practices* for a compliance program.

In a recent White Paper, entitled *"Staying out of the Headlines: Strategies to Combat Corruption Risk"* jointly produced by the consulting firm of Protiviti and the law firm of Covington and Burling, the authors reviewed 286 FCPA cases and analyzed the internal control weaknesses which led to FCPA enforcement actions. From this review, the authors derived a Top Five of Control Weaknesses. This article will review these findings and the authors' guidance on how a company might use this information to assist it to enhance its FCPA compliance program.

1. *Inadequate Contract Pricing Review*

The authors found that in 110 cases they reviewed, the internal controls were insufficient to confirm whether contract pricing was artificially inflated or otherwise altered. This enhanced the risk that a foreign business representative could inflate the price of goods and either keep the spread or use it to bribe a foreign governmental official. The types of internal controls weaknesses noted by the authors included:

- Inflated contract prices were used to generate and conceal kickbacks.
- Commissions were disguised as legitimate business expenses.
- Unwarranted additional fees were added to contract prices.

To remedy this contract pricing issue, the authors recommended that companies review their procurement policies from a FCPA compliance perspective. Companies should also engage in a competitive bidding process for purchases from third parties. Lastly invoices from third parties should provide sufficient detail to support the goods or services provided and back up for all expenses.

2. *Inadequate Due Diligence and Verification of Foreign Business Representative*

It is well known that companies are responsible for the actions of their business representatives and that this is a large source of FCPA exposure. Based upon their review, the authors found several examples of weaknesses in internal controls which led to FCPA enforcement actions. These weaknesses included:

- Monthly payments made to foreign business representatives where no written contract was in place.
- Contracts with foreign business representatives with prior histories of improper payments.
- Lack of vigorous due diligence based upon a valid risk analysis.

While noting the difficulties in the area of foreign business relationships, the authors proffer several steps to help ameliorate the risk. These steps include (1) a risk assessment and ranking of requisite due diligence based on this assessment; (2) collection, processing and analysis of information in a concise and effective manner; (3) confirm the business purpose, and indeed business need, for the third parties; (4) have a high level management review of all high risk foreign business partners; (5) include in your written contract, FCPA terms and conditions, including an affirmation of FCPA compliance; and (6) manage the foreign business partner relationship with an internal management sponsor.

3. Ineffective Accounts Payable Payment and Review

This area involves the review and appropriate authorization of funds prior to disbursement. The authors noted that vendor set up and management procedures were not well documented in the cases they reviewed and that company processes across wide geographic areas may not have the appropriate "checks and balances." The authors found the following internal control weaknesses in this area:

- Inappropriate payments made to agents under the guise of commissions, fees or legal services.
- Payments for professional services where no back up was provided by the vendor.
- Services were paid under contracts where such services were not addressed.

As remedies for these issues, the authors suggested that the classification of payments is critical. Additionally, supporting documentation must be a part of any request for payment but there must be an appropriate review and approval process followed for any disbursements. Finally, purchase orders must be matched with contracts for validation prior to payment.

4. Ineffective Financial Account Reconciliation and Review

The books and records component of the FCPA, together with the accounting control provisions, mandate that documentation on transactions must not only record the transaction but also adequately describe it to alert the reviewer to possible violations. In their analysis, the authors found several examples of ineffectual financial account reconciliation and review, which included:

- Inflated revenues through improper schemes.
- Recording of false entries by a subsidiary that was rolled up to a parent.
- False invoices were paid.
- Improper recordation of payments in various ledger accounts.
- Lack of appropriate documentation for disbursements.

The authors advised that companies should enhance financial reconciliation and review for FCPA compliance. Policies and procedures must be established and followed to help ensure accurate bookkeeping and accounting. Lastly, all transactions must have and be supported by appropriate documentation.

5. Ineffective Commission Payment Review and Authority

The authors noted instances of the lack of procedures to verify the payments of commissions to foreign business partners. These failures led to instances of bribery of a foreign governmental official by the foreign business partner. From their review the authors noted some of the following internal control weaknesses which led to a high number of enforcement cases in this area:

- Mission creep by foreign business partners in that the duties they carried out were not assigned within or by the contract.
- Misleading information was presented to company internal auditors regarding the amount of commissions paid by foreign business partners.
- Commission payments were inflated so that foreign business partners could provide kickbacks to foreign government officials.

To assist in this area the authors stressed the need for a review of all relevant information prior to making a commission payment. This would start with a review of the contract to ascertain if the agent was entitled to a commission, the amount of the commission and whether the work described met the contractual strictures. Care should be taken that all payments are made to the named contract counter-party and not an unnamed third party. The payment location should be verified to make certain no offshore payments are made. Lastly, the authors suggest training for any third party representatives to ensure their understanding of the requirements of the FCPA and any other relevant anti-bribery and anti-corruption laws applicable.

This White Paper is an excellent source of information the lack of internal controls which have led other companies into FCPA troubles. It provides some solid recommendations for the specific controls that a company should put into place. We commend the authors for their research and suggestions for *best practices* moving forward.

3. Oversight, Autonomy and Resources

Introduction

In a compliance program, a company should assign responsibility for the oversight and implementation of a company's compliance program to one or more specific senior executives within an organization. Those individuals must have appropriate authority within the organization, adequate autonomy from management, and sufficient resources to ensure that the company's compliance program is implemented effectively. Further, adequate autonomy should also include direct access to an organization's governing authority, such as the board of directors and committees of the board of directors (e.g., the audit committee). There must also be active oversight and involvement of the board of directors or specifically designated board committee.

Five Essentials of a Chief Compliance Officer Position

Posted December 2, 2012

Most of Shakespeare's histories involve issues relating to kingship and how a king might reign. In some of the plays, such as Henry V, the example is of a positive nature. In others, such as Richard III, you may need to draw from the inverse to see how one should decidedly not govern. The tragedies tend to emphasize a tragic flaw which brings down someone who is not necessarily a king, such as Hamlet or Coriolanus.

What are some of the characteristics of the position of a Chief Compliance Officer (CCO) for a company subject to the Foreign Corrupt Practices Act (FCPA), UK Bribery Act or other international anti-bribery and anti-corruption laws? That question was recently explored in an article in the Society of Corporate Compliance and Ethics (SCCE) bi-monthly magazine, Compliance & Ethics Professional, in an article entitled *"Five essential features of the Chief Ethics and Compliance Officer position"*, by author Donna Boehme. She believes that while all CCO positions should be "fit-for-purpose" there are five essential features which are consistent to all such positions. They are as follows:

1.   *Independence*

It is incumbent that any CCO must have "sufficient authority and independence to oversee the integrity of the compliance program." Some indicia of independence would include a reporting line to the company's Board of Directors and Audit/Compliance Committee but more importantly "unfiltered" access to the Board. There should also be protection of employment including an employment contract with a "nondiscretionary escalation clause" and a requirement for Board approval for any change in the terms and conditions of employment, including termination. There must also be sufficient resources in the form of an independent budget and adequate staff to manage the overall compliance program.

2.   *Empowerment*

Boehme believes that a CCO must have "the appropriate unambiguous mandate, delegation of authority, senior-level positioning, and empowerment to carry out his/her duties. Such can be accomplished through a "board resolution and a compliance charter, adopted by the board." Additionally, the CCO job description should be another manner in which to clarify the CCO "mandate, and at a minimum should encompass the single point accountability to develop, implement and oversee an effective compliance program." All of the above should lead in practice to a "close working relationship with an independent board committee."

3.   *Seat at the Table*

Boehme believes that the CCO must "have formal and informal connections into the business and functions of the organization – a seat at the table at important meetings where all major business matters (e.g., risk, major transactions, business plans) are discussed and decided." She argues that, at a minimum, the CCO should participate in "budget reviews, strategic planning meetings, disclosure committee meetings, operational reviews, and risk and crisis management meetings."

4.   *Line of Sight*

Here the author urges that the CCO should have "unfettered access to relevant information to be able to form independent opinions and manage the [compliance] program effectively." This does not mean that the CCO should have veto power over functions such as safety or environmental or that such functions must report to the CCO, but unless there is visibility to the CCO for these risk areas, the CCO will not able to adequately assess and manage such risks from the compliance perspective. The correct structuring of the CCO role to allow it visibility into these areas will help the CCO coordinate compliance convergence training.

5.   *Resources*

It is absolutely mandatory that the CCO be given both the physical resources in terms of personnel and monetary resources to "get the job done." I have worked at places where the CCO had neither and the CCOs did not succeed because they never even had the chance to do so. Boehme focuses on both types of resources. Under monetary resources she points, as an indicia, to the independence of the CCO from the General Counsel (GC), "rather than a shared budget". This can also bleed over to 'headcount' and shared or dotted line reporting resources. There should be independent resources reporting into the compliance function.

Unlike Shakespeare's histories or tragedies, the author gives you her opinion on what the role of the CCO should consist of in today's compliance arena. Boehme's article is an excellent guide for the CCO or Compliance Professional to use in reviewing the situation in his or her company. Her five essential features are based on the Department of

Justice's (DOJ) thinking on the issue in the form of the US Sentencing Guidelines, FCPA enforcement actions and evolving best practices. If your company is not following these it may well not be deemed to have a commitment to compliance or meet the minimum best practices standards.

The CCO: Co-Equal to the General Counsel in the Eyes of the DOJ

Posted December 20, 2012

One of the items that the Department of Justice (DOJ) has increasingly focused on in its enforcement actions is the role of the Chief Compliance Officer (CCO) and whether this position has adequate staffing and resources to accomplish its mandated tasks in a minimum *best practices* compliance program under the Foreign Corrupt Practices Act (FCPA). In the recent Pfizer Deferred Prosecution Agreement (DPA), it stated regarding the CCO position (called Chief Compliance and Risk Officer) that:

> *Pfizer will:*
> a. *Maintain the appointment of a senior corporate executive with significant experience with compliance with the FCPA, including its anti-bribery, books and records, and internal controls provisions, as well as other applicable anticorruption laws and regulations (hereinafter "anti-corruption laws and regulations") to serve as Chief Compliance and Risk Officer. The Chief Compliance and Risk Officer will have reporting obligations directly to the Chief Executive Officer and periodic reporting obligations to the Audit Committee of the Board of Directors.*

Regarding the resources which should be dedicated to the compliance function, the Pfizer DPA stated:

> *Pfizer has committed and will continue the commitment of significantly enhanced resources for*

*the international functions of the Compliance
Division that have reporting obligations through the
Chief Compliance ...*

The Pfizer DPA is one in a line of DPAs and Non-Prosecution Agreements (NPAs) where the DOJ and the Securities and Exchange Commission (SEC) have made clear that the CCO must be a senior level employee within the company. I think that this requirement is absolutely mandatory to not only set the proper tone within a company but also to give the CCO and the compliance function the clout needed to implement, enhance and run a minimum *best practices* FCPA compliance program.

Indeed, in the recently released FCPA Guidance, the DOJ and SEC made clear that in appraising a compliance program; [we] "consider whether a company has assigned responsibility for the oversight and implementation of a company's compliance program to one or more specific senior executives within an organization. Those individuals ***must have appropriate authority within the organization***, adequate autonomy from management, and ***sufficient resources to ensure that the company's compliance program is implemented effectively***. Adequate autonomy generally includes direct access to an organization's governing authority, such as the board of directors and committees of the board of directors (e.g., the audit committee). Depending on the size and structure of an organization, it may be appropriate for day-to-day operational responsibility to be delegated to other specific individuals within a company. The DOJ and SEC recognize that the reporting structure will depend on the size and complexity of an organization. Moreover, the amount of resources devoted to compliance will depend on the company's size, complexity, industry, geographical reach, and risks associated with the business. In assessing whether a company has reasonable internal controls, the DOJ and SEC typically consider **whether the company devoted adequate staffing and resources** to the compliance program given the size, structure, and risk profile of the business." [*Emphasis supplied*]

I think that the DOJ and SEC are moving companies to not only have more robust compliance programs but the CCOs and their programs must be adequately situated within the organization and adequately funded. For CCOs I think that this means they should be at a level in the organization equal to the General Counsel (GC) and compensated at an amount equal to the GC. The reason is clear, the DOJ and SEC expect the compliance function to be a leadership function within the company's structure and given all the respect due such a position. The days where the compliance function is viewed as something other than legal work are long gone and companies need to have their CCOs at least equivalent to their GCs. I also think that this always means the CCO must sit on a company's Executive Leadership Team (ELT). Once again the reason is clear, Compliance must not only be shown to be Mission 1A (Safety being Mission 1) but the CCO can only manage the compliance risk if it has a seat at the executive leadership table.

These comments are consistent with the US Sentencing Guidelines which were revised in November 2010. In these revisions, there was a change in the reporting structure in corporations where the CCO reported to the GC rather than a committee on the Board of Directors. The change read "the individual...with operational responsibility for the compliance and ethics program...have direct reporting obligations to the governing authority or any appropriate subgroup... (e.g. an audit committee or the board of directors)". If a company has the CCO reporting to the GC, who then reports to the Board, such structure most probably no longer qualifies as an effective compliance and ethics program under the amended Sentencing Guidelines. The better practice would now appear to be that the CCO should be a direct report to the Board or appropriate subcommittee of the Board such as compliance or audit.

Equally important are the resources dedicated to the compliance function. My colleague Stephen Martin, a former state and US prosecutor, gives this rather straight-forward example of a question that a prosecutor would ask when confronted by a company that provides limited internal funding to the compliance function. He would ask how much does your company spend on yellow post-it notes (or paper clips or pens)? If the answer is significantly more funding than is afforded to the compliance function, his response would be "Which area is more mission-critical to complying with the FCPA; your compliance function or yellow post-it notes?"

The DOJ is clearly signally the increased importance of the CCO. The position should be viewed as co-equal to the GC. Just as clearly, the DOJ has signaled that an appropriate level of resources should be devoted to the compliance function. By following these evolving *best practices* you can add to the credibility of your defenses if your company becomes involved in a FCPA investigation or enforcement action.

20 Questions Directors Should Ask about Compliance Committees

Posted May 18, 2011

What are some of the questions that the Board of Directors should be asking? We posit that a large public company should have Compliance Sub-Committee of Board members. We list 20 questions below which reflect the oversight role of directors which includes asking senior management and themselves. The questions are not intended to be an exact checklist, but rather a way to provide insight and stimulate discussion on the topic of compliance. The questions provide directors with a basis for critically assessing the answers they get and digging deeper as necessary.

The comments summarize current thinking on the issues and the practices of leading organizations. Although the questions apply to most medium to large organizations, the answers will vary according to the size, complexity and sophistication of each individual organization.

Part I: Understanding the Role and Value of the Compliance Committee

1.   What are the Compliance Committee's responsibilities and what value does it bring to the board?
2.   How can the Compliance Committee help the board enhance its relationship with management?
3.   What is the role of the Compliance Committee?

Part II: Building an Effective Compliance Committee

4. What skill sets does the Compliance Committee require?
5. Who should sit on the Compliance Committee?
6. Who should chair the Compliance Committee?

Part III: Directed to the Board

7. What is the Compliance Committee's role in building an effective compliance program within the company?
8. How can the Compliance Committee assess potential members and senior leaders of the company's compliance program?
9. How long should directors serve on the Compliance Committee?
10. How can the Compliance Committee assist directors in retiring from the board?

Part IV: Enhancing the Board's Performance Effectiveness

11. How can the Compliance Committee assist in director development?
12. How can the Compliance Committee help the board chair sharpen the board's overall performance focus?
13. What is the Compliance Committee's role in board evaluation and feedback?
14. What should the Compliance Committee do if a director is not performing or not interacting effectively with other directors?
15. Should the Compliance Committee have a role in chair succession?

16.   How can the Compliance Committee help the board keep its mandates, policies and practices up-to-date?

Part V: Merging Roles of the Compliance Committees

17.   How can the Compliance Committee enhance the board's relationship with institutional shareholders and other stakeholders?
18.   What is the Compliance Committee's role in Chief Compliance Officer (CCO) succession?
19.   What role can the Compliance Committee play in preparing for a crisis, such as the discovery of a sign of a significant compliance violation?
20.   How can the Compliance Committee help the board in deciding CCO pay and bonus?

We hope these questions may lead to further discussions and debate on the role of the Board in a company's overall compliance program. We invite any reader to comment on these and add their own questions which may lead to further dialogue and inquiry for a Board or Compliance Committee.

4. Risk Assessment

<u>Introduction</u>

A risk assessment is fundamental to the development of a strong ethics and compliance program. Factors to consider, in a risk assessment, should include the following: risks presented by the country and industry sector, the business opportunity, potential business partners, level of involvement with governments, amount of government regulation and oversight, and exposure to customs and immigration in conducting business affairs. When assessing a company's compliance program, the US Department of Justice (DOJ) and the Securities and Exchange Commission (SEC) take into account whether and to what degree a company analyzes and addresses the particular risks it faces.

FCPA Risk Assessments: New Input into Current Best Practices

Posted February 16, 2011

We believe that Risk Assessment is a tool and is one with which a company should begin to craft its Foreign Corrupt Practices (FCPA) or UK Bribery Act compliance program. The simple reason is straightforward; one cannot define, plan for, or design an effective compliance program to prevent bribery and corruption unless you can measure the risks you face. Both the both the Principles of Federal Prosecution of Business Organization (US Sentencing Guidelines) and its section on corporate compliance programs and the UK Bribery Act's Consultative Guidance list Risk Assessment as the initial step in creating an effective anti-corruption and anti-bribery program. So far, in 2011 the US Department of Justice (DOJ) has concluded three FCPA enforcement actions which specify some factors which a company should review when making a Risk Assessment.

The three enforcement actions, involving the companies Alcatel-Lucent, Maxwell Technologies and Tyson Foods all had common areas that the DOJ indicated were FCPA compliance risk areas which should be evaluated for a minimum *best practices* FCPA compliance program. In both Alcatel-Lucent and Maxwell Technologies, the Deferred Prosecution Agreements (DPAs) listed the seven following areas of risk to be assessed.

    1.   Geography - Where does your Company do business?
    2.   Interaction with types and levels of Governments.
    3.   Industrial Sector of Operations.

4.   Involvement with Joint Ventures.
5.   Licenses and Permits in Operations.
6.   Degree of Government Oversight.
7.   Volume and Importance of Goods and Personnel Going Through Customs and Immigration.

In the Tyson Foods DPA, this list was reduced to the following (1) Geography, (2) Interaction with Governments, and (3) Industrial Sector of Operations. It would seem that the DOJ did not believe that Tyson Foods had the same compliance risks as Alcatel-Lucent and Maxwell Technologies because (a) their limited internal sales market and (b) the fact it only has 6 food processing plants outside the United States.

These factors provide guidance into some of the key areas that the DOJ apparently believes can put a company at higher FCPA risk. These factors supplement those listed in the UK Bribery, Consultative Guidance which states, "Risk Assessment - The commercial organization regularly and comprehensively assesses the nature and extent of the risks relating to bribery to which it is exposed." The Guidance points towards several key risks which should be evaluated in this process. These risk areas include:

1.   Internal Risk - this could include deficiencies in
      • employee knowledge of a company's business profile and understanding of associated bribery and corruption risks;
      • employee training or skills sets; and
      • the company's compensation structure or lack of clarity in the policy on gifts, entertaining and travel expenses.

2. <u>Country risk</u> – this type of risk could include:

   (a) perceived high levels of corruption as highlighted by corruption league tables published by reputable Non-Governmental Organizations such as Transparency International;

   (b) factors such as absence of anti-bribery legislation and implementation and a perceived lack of capacity of the government, media, local business community and civil society to effectively promote transparent procurement and investment policies; and

   (c) a culture which does not punish those who seek bribes or make other extortion attempts.

3. <u>Transaction Risk</u> – this could entail items such as transactions involving charitable or political contributions, the obtaining of licenses and permits, public procurement, high value or projects with many contractors or involvement of intermediaries or agents.

4. <u>Partnership risks</u> – this risk could include those involving foreign business partners located in higher-risk jurisdictions, associations with prominent public office holders, insufficient knowledge or transparency of third party processes and controls.

Risk Assessment as 'Best Practices'

Both the Consultative Guidance and the recent DPAs provide guidance to the FCPA compliance practitioner and include ongoing Risk Assessment as a key component of any *best practices* program. A well-managed organization makes an assessment of the risks it faces now and in the future and then designs appropriate risk management and control mechanisms to control such risks. However, the key point is that a Risk Assessment is absolutely mandatory and must be used as a basis for the design of an effective compliance policy, whether under the FCPA or the UK Bribery Act. If a Risk Assessment is not used, it might be well-nigh impossible to argue that your compliance program meets even the basic standards of either law.

How To Risk-Base Supply Chain Vendors Under The FCPA

Posted November 16, 2010

What are the methods to assess the risks of your Supply Chain vendors? Other than perhaps financial due diligence, such as through Dun & Bradstreet or quality control through your QHSE group, the Supply Chain probably does not command your Compliance Department's attention as do other types of third party business partners such as agents, distributors and joint venture (JV) partners. This may be coming to an end as most Compliance Professionals recognize that third parties which supply goods or services to a company should be scrutinized similarly to other third party business partners. In the recently released Deferred Prosecution Agreement (DPA) with Panalpina and six other oil-field service companies, the Department of Justice (DOJ) specifically noted that regarding business partners, such as Supply Chain vendors, a company "should institute appropriate due diligence" so as to help ensure compliance with the US Foreign Corrupt Practices Act (FCPA).

However, to initiate "appropriate due diligence" a company must first rate the compliance risk of any third party, such as a Supply Chain vendor. The risk rating will inform the level of due diligence required. There are several methods that could be used to assess risk in the area of supply chain and vendors. The approach suggested by the UK's Financial Services Authority (FSA) in its settlement of the enforcement action against the insurance giant AON would refer "to an internationally accepted corruption perceptions index" such as is available through Transparency International (TI) or other recognized authority. The approach suggested by the DOJ, in Opinion Release 08-02, would provide categories of "High Risk, Medium Risk and Low Risk". Finally, writing in the FCPA Blog, Scott Moritz of Daylight Forensic & Advisory LLC has suggested an approach that incorporates a variety of risk-assessment tools, including, "the strategic use of information technology, tracking and sorting the critical elements".

This commentary proposes an approach which would incorporate all three of the above cited analogous compliance areas into one risk-based assessment program for supply chain vendors. Based upon the assessed risk, an appropriate level of due diligence would then be required. The categories suggested are as follows:

1. High Risk Suppliers;
2. Low Risk Suppliers;
3. Nominal Risk Suppliers; and
4. Suppliers of General Goods and Products.

A.   High-Risk Suppliers

A High-Risk Supplier is defined as a supplier which presents a higher level of compliance risk because of the presence of one or more of the following factors:

1. It is based in or supplies goods/services from a high risk country;
2. It has a reputation in the business community for questionable business practices or ethics; or
3. It has been convicted of, or is alleged to have been involved in, illegal conduct and has failed to undertake effective remedial actions.

B. Low-Risk Suppliers

A Low-Risk Supplier is defined as an individual or private entity located in a Low-Risk Country which:

1. Supplies goods or services in a Low-Risk Country;
2. Is based in a low risk country where the goods or services are delivered, it has no involvement with any foreign government, government entity, or Government Official; or
3. Is subject to the US FCPA and/or Sarbanes-Oxley compliance.

C. Minimal-Risk Suppliers

A Minimal-Risk Supplier is an individual or entity which provides goods or services that are non-specific to a particular job or assignment and the value of each transaction is USD $10,000 or less. These types of vendors include office and industrial suppliers, equipment leasing companies and such entities which supply such routinely used services.

D. Suppliers of General Goods and Products

A Supplier of General Goods and Products is an individual or entity which provides goods or services that are widely available to the general public and do not fall under the definition of Minimal-Risk Supplier. These types of vendors include transportation, food services and educational services providers.

This proposed rating is but one method to allow a company to assess its risks involving its Supply Chain vendors. As has been noted in both the Consultative Guidance to the UK Bribery Act and in the Panalpina settlements, both documents list the risk rating as a key component of a *best practices* anti-corruption and anti-bribery compliance program. A company need not engage in full due diligence for all Supply Chain vendors, however it must implement and follow a system to rate each vendor for that vendor's FCPA compliance risk and evaluate and manage that relationship accordingly.

5. Training and Continuing Advice

Introduction

Compliance policies cannot work unless effectively communicated throughout a company. This means that a company must take steps to ensure that relevant policies and procedures have been communicated throughout the organization, including through periodic training and certification for all directors, officers, relevant employees, and, where appropriate, agents and business partners. Training should encompass policies and procedures, instruction on applicable laws, practical advice to address real-life scenarios, and case studies. The information should be presented in a manner appropriate for the targeted audience, including providing training and training materials in the local language. In addition to training, a company should develop appropriate measures, depending on the size and sophistication of the particular company, to provide guidance and advice on complying with the company's ethics and compliance program, including when such advice is needed urgently.

End of the Annual Compliance and Ethics Training 'Flea Dip'

Posted August 9, 2011

In an article in the July/August edition of the ACC Docket entitled *"Rethinking the Annual Compliance and Ethics Flea Dip"*, author James Nortz discusses the annual compliance and ethics training program that most US company's employees receive which he calls a *'flea dip'*. While he believes that such annual training is well-intentioned, he states that it is "a bit implausible that these annual pilgrimages" would have their intended effect of raising overall employee aware of their company's Code of Conduct and thereby reducing overall enterprise compliance risks.

Nortz cites two major reasons for this educational failure. The first is that "most compliance and ethics presentations anesthetize all but the most caffeinated, and are utterly unforgettable." To drive this point home, he challenges the reader to recall "even one PowerPoint slide" of the most recent compliance and ethics training presentation that they may have attended. The second reason is to truly affect behavior and get employees to understand the relevance of company Codes of Conduct, Nortz believes that a "different approach to teaching and learning is required." He believes that "the recently developed 'Learning IFF Action Model' may provide" a better method for success in compliance and ethics training.

He defines 'IFF' as "learning *in, from* and *for* action." In the IFF model, teaching is rooted in "both cognitive learning theory and common sense." Under this teaching theory, real-life experiences are incorporated into classroom training to reflect employees experiences out in the business world. Nortz believes that such training is more beneficial in the compliance and ethics arena "where old habits are difficult to change and the application of even simple rules to circumstances that arise in the workplace can present complex, difficult challenges."

Nortz suggests moving away from a full and thorough discussion of relevant laws, whether they are your company's internal Code of Conduct or the Foreign Corrupt Practices Act (FCPA). He also suggests that compliance and ethics training should be integrated into more routine employee training rather than standalone compliance and ethics training. The more innovative component of Nortz's suggestions revolves around employee involvement and follow up. He believes that employees should be encouraged to share their experiences of how a company's Code of Conduct "come into play and affect the way they do their jobs" with other employees. The second component is to require employees, at periodic intervals, to meet with one another and their direct managers "to reflect and discuss how they handled particular situations in which the company Code of Conduct may have come into place". He re-emphasizes that such discussions can be best held in a routine business meeting and not to wait for any annual compliance and ethics training.

Nortz ends by noting that the IFF approach will require "considerably more thought and energy" than the traditional training approach which involves using PowerPoint slides as the primary training materials. He ends by stating that "if you are truly interested in ridding your company of 'fleas', it may be a good idea to try an approach like the IFF learning model, which provides a more reasonable prospect of actually working."

While I would certainly urge that a full and thorough discussion of the relevant laws is useful, a training written by lawyers for lawyers will have the eyes of the business team rolled up in their collective heads within 30 minutes. You do need to do something to make the training memorable. Nortz's suggestion of an IFF type approach is something which will make your compliance and ethics training more relevant and certainly more noteworthy.

FCPA Training: Some Practical Aspects of Resisting a Bribe

Posted July 13, 2011

I recently was asked to prepare some Foreign Corrupt Practices Act (FCPA) training which used examples of requests for bribes to help prepare the company's employees if they are solicited to pay a bribe. To do so I relied on the expanded edition of *Resisting Extortion and Solicitation in International Transactions* (RESIST). It is a practical tool to help companies train employees to respond appropriately to a variety of solicitations.

Iohann Le Frapper, who chaired the RESIST initiative, stated that "RESIST is the only anti-bribery training toolkit developed by companies for companies and sponsored by the four global anti-corruption initiatives working on the supply side of the issue of fighting corruption," and it "helps businesses avoid solicitation from the onset"; it also provides practical advice on how best to confront demands for bribes when they do arise.

RESIST presents 22 scenarios which discuss solicitation of bribes in the context of project implementation and in day-to-day project operations. Each scenario presented is designed to respond to two basic questions with real world facts and responses:

- Demand Prevention - How can the company prevent the demand from being made in the first place?
- Demand Response - How should the company react if such a demand is made?

The paper also presents a general list of suggestions which companies can implement to assist in their overall FCPA compliance effort. Embedded within are specific procedures to put these general suggestions into practice, for example the suggestions on Demand Prevention include (1) general company anti-corruption polices; (2) policies on facilitation payments; (3) policies for company representatives who may be exposed to solicitation of bribes; (4) techniques for dealing with specific risks; (5) due diligence of agents and intermediaries; (6) management of agents and intermediaries; (7) implementation of additional control procedures; (8) transparency in the procurement process; (9) initiation of collective action to improve overall business integrity; and (10) implementation of legal and financial precautions. The suggestions on Demand Response include: (1) the immediate response; (2) internal company reporting; (3) company investigation, including discussion with the relevant persons; (4) disclose to the appropriate external source, if appropriate; and ultimately (5) withdrawal from the situation, whether it is the project or the entire country.

Using the RESIST scenarios I was able to create training which many of the participants felt gave them some hands on advice in situations they might face. It fleshed out many of what the employees felt were the more theoretical aspects of the FCPA. The RESIST tool is a useful aid and one that I recommend for the FCPA compliance specialist. It provides a list of common scenarios, which companies have faced in the past, how to handle them and proposes controls to implement to try and ameliorate the solicitation of bribes and outright extortion.

6. Incentives and Disciplinary Measures

Introduction

As the FCPA Guidance notes, a company's ethics and compliance program should apply "from the board room to the supply room—no one should be beyond its reach." This means that if there is a violation of the company's ethics and compliance program, a company must have disciplinary action procedures in place and utilize them, where appropriate. Such discipline should be enforced fairly and promptly and should be commensurate with the violation. Moreover, beyond the simple stick of discipline, a company should also have positive benefits in place for adherence to its ethics and compliance program. Such incentives can include personnel evaluations and promotions, rewards for improving and developing a company's compliance program, and rewards for ethics and compliance leadership. But whatever discipline and incentives that a company decides to adopt, it must be fair and consistently across the organization.

Using HR to Change your Company's Compliance DNA

Posted August 23, 2011

In his Editor's View column in the August issue of Compliance Week, entitled *"Compliance, Collaboration and HR"*, Matt Kelly wrote about the interaction of Compliance Departments and Human Resources (HR). He noted that while Compliance Departments may look to HR to support internal investigations, HR can also be used to assist in "molding company culture." However, it is rarely used for this function. I heartily agree with Matt's sentiments. In addition to supporting internal investigations, I believe that HR can be used in some of the following ways to assist the Compliance Department. It can be a key component in changing or maintaining your company's compliance DNA.

Training

A key role for HR in any company is training. This has traditionally been in areas such as discrimination, harassment and safety, to name just a few, and, based on this traditional role of HR in training, this commentator would submit that it is a natural extension for HR's function to expand to the area of Foreign Corrupt Practices Act (FCPA) compliance and ethics training. There is a training requirement set forth in the US Sentencing Guidelines and companies are mandated to *"take reasonable steps to communicate periodically and in a practical manner its standards and procedures, and other aspects of the compliance and ethics program, to the individuals referred to in subdivision (B) by conducting effective training programs and otherwise disseminating information appropriate to such individuals' respective roles and responsibilities."*

What type of training should HR utilize in the FCPA compliance and ethics arena? The consensus seems to be that there are three general approaches which have been used successfully. The first is the most traditional and that is in-person classroom training. This gives employees an opportunity to see, meet and interact directly with the trainer, not an insignificant dynamic in the corporate environment. It can also lead to confidential discussions after such in-person training. All FCPA compliance and ethics training should be coordinated and both the attendance and result recorded. Results can be tabulated through short questionnaires immediately following the training and bench-marked through more comprehensive interviewing of selected training participants to determine overall effectiveness.

Employee Evaluation and Succession Planning

What policy does a company take to punish those employees who may engage in unethical and non-compliant behavior in order to meet company revenue targets? Conversely, what rewards are handed out to those employees who integrate such ethical and compliant behavior into their individual work practices going forward? One of the very important functions of HR is assisting management in setting the criteria for employee bonuses and in the evaluation of employees for those bonuses. This is an equally important role in conveying the company message of adherence to a FCPA compliance and ethics policy. This requirement is codified in the US Sentencing Guidelines with the following language: *"The organization's compliance and ethics program shall be promoted and enforced consistently throughout the organization through (A) appropriate incentives to perform in accordance with the compliance and ethics program; and (B) appropriate disciplinary measures for engaging in criminal conduct and for failing to take reasonable steps to prevent or detect criminal conduct."*

Does a company have, as a component of its bonus compensation plan, a part dedicated to FCPA compliance and ethics? If so, how is this component measured and then administered? There is very little in the corporate world that an employee notices more than what goes into the calculation of their bonuses. HR can, and should, facilitate this process by setting expectations early in the year and then following through when bonuses are released. With the assistance of HR, such a bonus can send a powerful message to employees regarding the seriousness with which compliance is taken at the company. There is nothing like putting your money where your mouth is for people to stand up and take notice.

In addition to employee evaluation, HR can play a key role in assisting a company to identify early on in an employee's career the propensity for compliance and ethics by focusing on leadership behaviors in addition to simply business excellence. If a company has an employee who meets, or exceeds, all his sales targets, but does so in a manner which is opposite to the company's stated FCPA compliance and ethics values, other employees will watch and see how that employee is treated. Is that employee rewarded with a large bonus? Is that employee promoted or are the employee's violations of the company's compliance and ethics policies swept under the carpet? If the employee is rewarded, both monetarily and through promotions, or in any way not sanctioned for unethical or non-compliant behavior, it will be noticed and other employees will act accordingly. One of the functions of HR is to help ensure consistent application of company values throughout the organization, including those identified as 'rising stars'. An important role of HR in any organization is to help in building trust throughout the company and recognizing the benefits which result from that trust.

Background Screening

A key role for HR in any company is the background screening of not only employees at the time of hire, but also of employees who may be promoted to senior leadership positions. HR is usually on the front lines of such activities, although it may in conjunction with the Legal or Compliance Departments. This requirement is discussed in the US Federal Sentencing Guidelines for Organizations (FSGO) as follows *"The organization shall use reasonable efforts not to include within the substantial authority personnel of the organization any individual whom the organization knew, or should have known through the exercise of due diligence, has engaged in illegal activities or other conduct inconsistent with an effective compliance and ethics program."*

What type of background checks should HR utilize in the FCPA compliance and ethics arena? The consensus seems to be that HR should perform at least routine civil, criminal and credit background checks. Care should be noted in any such request made in countries outside the United States as such information may be protected by privacy laws or where the quality of such information is different in substance from that of the United States. For instance in the United Kingdom, the request of a credit check can negatively impact a prospective employee's credit score so such a background check may not provide useful information to a prospective employer.

Additionally, although it may be difficult in the United States to do so, a thorough check of references should be made. I say that it may be difficult because many companies will only confirm that the employee worked at the company and only give out the additional information of dates of employment. In this situation, it may be that a prospective employer should utilize a current employee to contact former associates at other companies to get a sense of the prospective employee's business ethics. However, it should be noted that such contacts should only be made after a thorough briefing by HR of the current employee who might be asked to perform such duty.

A company can also use HR to perform internal background checks on employees who may be targeted for promotions. These types of internal background checks can include a detailed review of employee performance; disciplinary actions, if any; internal and external achievements, while employed by the company and confirmation of both ethics and compliance training and that the employee has completed the required annual compliance certification. A key internal function where HR can be an important lead is to emphasize that an employee, who has been investigated but cleared of any alleged ethics and compliance violations, should not be penalized.

When the Government Comes Calling

While it is true that a company's Legal and/or Compliance Department will lead the response to a government investigation, HR can fulfill an important support role due to the fact that HR should maintain, as part of its routine function, a hard copy of many of the records which may need to be produced in such an investigation. This would include all pre-employment screening documents, including background investigations, all post-employment documents, including any additional screening documents, compliance training and testing thereon and annual compliance certifications. HR can be critical in identifying and tracking down former employees. HR will work with Legal and/or Compliance to establish protocols for the conduct of investigations and who should be involved.

Lastly, another role for HR can be in the establishment and management of (1) an Amnesty Program or (2) a Leniency Program for both current, and former, employees. Such programs were implemented by Siemens during its internal bribery and corruption investigation. The Amnesty Program allowed appropriate current or former employees, who fully cooperated and provided truthful information, to be relieved from the prospect of civil damage claims or termination. The Leniency Program allowed Siemens employees who had provided untrue information in the investigation to correct this information for certain specific discipline. Whichever of these programs, or any variations, that are implemented HR can perform a valuable support role to Legal and/or Compliance.

Doing More with Less

While many practitioners do not immediately consider HR as a key component of a FCPA compliance solution, it can be one of the lynch-pins in spreading a company's commitment to compliance throughout the employee base. HR can also be used to 'connect the dots' in many divergent elements in a company's FCPA compliance and ethics program. The roles listed for HR in this series are functions that HR currently performs for almost any US company with international operations. By asking HR to expand their traditional function to include the FCPA compliance and ethics function, a US company can move towards a goal of a more complete compliance program, while not significantly increasing costs. Additionally, by asking HR to include these functions, it will drive home the message of compliance to all levels within a company; from senior to middle management and to those on the shop floor. Just as safety is usually message Number 1, compliance can be message Number 1A. HR focuses on behaviors, and by asking this department to include a compliance and ethics message, such behavior will become a part of a company's DNA.

Henry II Revisited: The Fair Process Doctrine as a Key Component of a Compliance Program

Posted August 15, 2011

In a recent post entitled *"Will No One Rid Me of this Meddlesome Priest?"* I highlighted 'Tone at the Top' by discussing the words of Henry II leading to the subsequent murder of Thomas Becket. One of the things I learned on my recent vacation to England was that Henry II developed many of the procedural safeguards which became the basis of Anglo-American jurisprudence. While English Kings, at least after William the Conqueror, had always been able to issue Writs to direct the King's subjects to perform tasks, Henry II developed certain standardized Writs which could be utilized to determine disputes between the King's subjects, in a more fair and judicial manner. So today we will honor Henry II by discussing how he helped to bring procedural fairness to English law and how that relates to modern day compliance program.

Two of the most famous were the *Writ of Novel Disseisin*, which would allow a person to contest property ownership through a trial on the merits, decided by a jury. The second was a *Writ of Mort D'Ancestor* which allowed heirs to contest property distribution after a person's death. As with the *Writ of Novel Disseisin*, it would be issued in the King's name to the County Sheriff, who would seize the property in question. The matter would then go through a legal process culminating in a trial by jury to determine rightful ownership. Both of these Writs allowed a manner of procedural fairness to come into disputes which heretofore had not been present in English law.

Procedural fairness is one of the things that will bring credibility to your Compliance Program. Today it is called the Fair Process Doctrine and this Doctrine generally recognizes that there are fair procedures, not arbitrary ones, in processes involving rights. Considerable research has shown that people are more willing to accept negative, unfavorable, and non-preferred outcomes when they are arrived at by processes and procedures that are perceived as fair. Adhering to the Fair Process Doctrine in two areas of your Compliance Program is critical for you, as a compliance specialist or for your Compliance Department, to have credibility with the rest of the workforce.

A. Internal Investigations

The first area is that of internal company investigations. If your employees do not believe that the investigation is fair and impartial, then it is not fair and impartial. Further, those involved must have confidence that any internal investigation is treated seriously and objectively. I have recently written about several aspects of internal investigations, in order to emphasize how to handle internal whistleblower complaints in light of the Dodd-Frank implications. One of the key reasons that employees will go outside of a company's internal hotline process is because they do not believe that the process will be fair.

This fairness has several components. One would be the use of outside counsel, rather than in-house counsel to handle the investigation. Moreover, if company uses a regular firm, it may be that other outside counsel should be brought in, particularly if regular outside counsel has created or implemented key components which are being investigated. Further, if the company's regular outside counsel has a large amount of business with the company, then that law firm may have a very vested interest in maintaining the status quo. Lastly, the investigation may require a level of specialization which in-house or regular outside counsel does not possess.

B. *Administration of Discipline and Employee Promotions*

However, as important as the Fair Process Doctrine is with internal investigations, I have come to believe it is more important in another area. That area is in the administration of discipline after any compliance related incident. Discipline must not only be administered fairly but it must be administered uniformly across the company for the violation of any compliance policy. Simply put if you are going to fire employees in South America for lying on their expense reports, you have to fire them in North America for the same offense. It cannot matter that the North American employee is a friend of yours or worse yet a 'high producer'. Failure to administer discipline uniformly will destroy any vestige of credibility that you may have developed.

In addition to the area of discipline which may be administered after the completion of any compliance investigation, you must also place compliance firmly as a part of ongoing employee evaluations and promotions. If your company is seen to advance and only reward employees who achieve their numbers by whatever means necessary, other employees will certainly take note and it will be understood what management evaluates, and rewards, employees upon. I have often heard the (anecdotal) tale about some Far East Region Manager which goes along the following lines *"If I violated the Code of Conduct I may or may not get caught. If I get caught I may or may not be disciplined. If I miss my numbers for two quarters, I will be fired"*. If this is what other employees believe about how they are evaluated and the basis for promotion, you have lost the compliance battle.

So we should thank Henry II for showing us that he was more than simply about 'Tone at the Top'. His changes in English jurisprudence helped lead us down the road to procedural fairness in the law and today in the workplace. You should thank him and remember that people will be more loyal if they think they have been treated fairly, even if the results are not exactly what they wanted.

7. Third Party Due Diligence and Payments

Introduction

The use of third parties has been the single highest cause for Foreign Corrupt Practice Act (FCPA) violations over the years. Companies must carefully assess who they are doing business with, how that business is conducted and monitored. The FCPA Guidance specifies three areas for due diligence of third parties. *(1) Risk Based Due Diligence.* Companies need to understand the qualifications and associations of its third-party partners, including its business reputation, and relationship, if any, with foreign officials. The degree of scrutiny should increase as red flags surface. *(2) Evaluation of the Due Diligence.* A company needs to have an understanding of the business rationale for including the third party in the transaction and ensure that the contract terms specifically describe the services to be performed. *(3) Ongoing Monitoring of the Third Party.* Care should be taken to confirm and document that the third party is actually performing the work for which it is being paid and that its compensation is commensurate with the work being provided. Such monitoring should also include updating due diligence periodically, exercising audit rights, providing periodic training, and requesting annual compliance certifications by the third party.

Tyco's Seven Step Process for Third Party Qualification

Posted December 1, 2011

An article in the September, 2011 issue of Compliance Week, entitled *"How Tyco Turned Around Third-Party Risk Program"*, by author Karen Kroll who reported on the program initiated and developed by Tyco International Ltd (Tyco), assisted by Navigant Consulting, to enable Tyco to develop and initiate a "comprehensive program to gain a better control over the activities of third parties." This task seemed particularly daunting as Tyco initially identified over 66,000+ third party vendors and this group needed to be risk assessed to determine the high risk third parties which could be handled in the first pass.

Key First Step

Interestingly a key first step in the process was that Tyco set up a specific project team in the company to handle the task. This is different to such assignments in a Compliance or Legal Department where a project is added to an employee's existing portfolio of assignments. The Chief Compliance Counsel (CCO), Matthew Tanzer made the decision to assign a "small group of dedicated employees to the job". Scott Moritz, Managing Director of Navigant, who worked with Tyco on the project, said this was an important early decision and was quoted as saying "You need to develop bench strength to deal with this, and staffing that's proportional to the third party population."

The Seven Steps

Tyco developed a process to identify, risk assess, contract with and then compliance train its third parties in this project. Tyco distilled this process into the following seven steps.

1. **Business Sponsor:** Initially identify a business sponsor or primary contact for the third party within your company. This requires not only business unit buy-in but business unit accountability for the business relationship or as Moritz was quoted as saying, "This puts the onus on each stakeholder."

2. **Business Justification:** The business unit must articulate a commercial reason to initiate or continue to work with the third party. You need to determine how this third party will fit into your company's value chain and whether they will become a strategic partner or will they be involved in a one-off only transaction?

3. **Third-Party Questionnaire:** This requirement is not only a key step but a mandatory step for any third party which desire to do work with your company. I tell clients that if a third party does not want to fill out the questionnaire or will not fill it out completely that you should not walk but run away from doing business with such a party. The minimum information which should be obtained is basic business information, disclosures of all direct and beneficial owners, politically exposed persons (PEPs) and both commercial and compliance references.

4. **FCPA Certification:** You should require a representative of the third party to attest that it will comply with all relevant anti-corruption laws and will not pay bribes, "either directly or indirectly."

5. **Risk Assessment**: The above information should be analyzed which leads to a risk score. This risk assessment will be used to determine the appropriate level of due diligence that should be performed on the third party. In Tyco's system, the higher the risk assessment score, the more due diligence should be performed.
6. **Written Agreements:** This requirement mandates that, in addition to commercial terms, compliance terms and conditions are appended to each third party contract. This is now Item 12 in the Department of Justice's (DOJ) minimum *best practices* as set out in Deferred Prosecution Agreements (DPA) since at least November 2010.
7. **Training:** Your company should require all third parties to complete an online training module which discusses your company's values and its approach to bribery and corruption. You should also consider live training for the highest risk third parties.

The Tyco Seven Step Process does end at training though Tyco continues to manage these risks through an ongoing monitoring program which they developed in the course of this exercise. This monitoring includes both substantive compliance and transactional monitoring. Both of these monitoring systems can be reviewed by a committee or group dedicated to ongoing management of third parties within Tyco.

The task of getting a handle on your company's third parties may often seem daunting. However, the Tyco Seven Step Process provides an excellent framework for the compliance professional to develop a program for his/her company.

FCPA Compliance Contract Template

Post September 28, 2010

Speaking at the Seventh Annual IQPC Advanced Contracts Risks Management for Oil and Gas Conference, Don Butler, General Counsel (GC), Seneca Resources discussed contract templates and the use of these documents in transactional work. The concepts which Mr. Butler discussed are applicable when drafting templates which include language related to Foreign Corrupt Practices Act (FCPA) contractual terms.

He began his presentation by noting that by use of the word 'template' he meant that it was a form of contract drafted by his company for use in certain transactions. It was designed to be more than just a starting point for negotiations. The template has several benefits for Seneca which, as he related, include: (1) the language is tested against real events; (2) the language assists the company in managing its risks; (3) the language fits into a series of related contracts; (4) the language is straight-forward to administer and (5) the language helps to manage the expectations of both contracting parties.

The contracting concepts are equally applicable to contracts which a company, subject to the FCPA or UK Bribery Act, would enter into with a Foreign Business Partner such as an agent, distributor, reseller, joint venture partner or any other person or entity which might represent a US or UK business internationally. Such templates must have compliance obligations stated directly in the document, whether such document is a simple agency or consulting agreement or a joint venture with several formation documents. The FCPA compliance language should include representations that in all undertakings the Foreign

Business Partner will make no payments of money, or anything of value, nor will such be offered, promised or paid, directly or indirectly, to any foreign officials, political parties, party officials, candidates for public or political party office, to influence the acts of such officials, political parties, party officials, or candidates in their official capacity, to induce them to use their influence with a government to obtain or retain business or gain an improper advantage in connection with any business venture or contract in which the Company is a participant.

In addition to the above affirmative statements regarding conduct, a FCPA contract template should have the following compliance terms and conditions in a Foreign Business Partner contract.

- **Indemnification:** Full indemnification for any FCPA violation, including all costs for the underlying investigation.
- **Cooperation:** Require full cooperation with any ethics and compliance investigation, specifically including the review of Foreign Business Partner emails and bank accounts relating to your Company's use of the Foreign Business Partner.
- **Material Breach of Contract:** Any FCPA violation is made a material breach of contract, with no notice and opportunity to cure. Further, such a finding will be the grounds for immediate cessation of all payments.
- **No Sub-Vendors (without approval):** The Foreign Business Partner must agree that it will not hire an agent, subcontractor or consultant without the Company's prior written consent (to be based on adequate due diligence).

- **Audit Rights:** An additional key element of a contract between a US Company and a Foreign Business Partner should include the retention of audit rights. These audit rights must exceed the simple audit rights associated with the financial relationship between the parties and must allow a full review of all FCPA related compliance procedures such as those for meeting with foreign governmental officials and compliance related training.
- **Acknowledgment:** The Foreign Business Partner should specifically acknowledge the applicability of the FCPA to the business relationship as well as any country or regional anti-corruption or anti-bribery laws which apply to either the Foreign Business Partner or business relationship.
- **On-going Training:** Require that the top management of the Foreign Business Partner and all persons performing services on your behalf shall receive FCPA compliance training.
- **Annual Certification:** Require an annual certification stating that the Foreign Business Partner has not engaged in any conduct that violates the FCPA or any applicable laws, nor is it aware of any such conduct.
- **Re-qualification:** Require the Foreign Business Partner re-qualify as a business partner at a regular interval of no greater than every three years.

Traditional contracting techniques are a useful tool in the FCPA contracting area. By having such template language, a company can put forward the compliance terms and conditions which will not only communicate the Foreign Business Partner's FCPA compliance obligations but also to protect a business, to the highest degree possible, through risk shifting-clauses.

So what is in your FCPA contract template?

Foreign Joint Ventures: Dennis Haist and Some Characteristics of FCPA Risk

Posted February 18, 2011

In an article in the January/February issue of the ACC Docket, entitled *"Guilt by Association: Transnational Joint Ventures and the FCPA"*; Dennis Haist, General Counsel (GC) of The Steele Foundation (Steele) discussed some of the risks US companies can encounter under the Foreign Corrupt Practices Act (FCPA) when doing business overseas through the vehicle of a Joint Venture (JV). After an introduction of the increasing risks to US companies for FCPA enforcement by reviewing some recent Department of Justice (DOJ) enforcement actions, Haist reviews some of the characteristics which may increase FCPA risk. We found his list to be a useful resource in thinking through FCPA compliance. The listed included the following:

1. **Sharing of Risk/Reward**. The commingling of risk and reward by the joint venture participants. Most generally, a transnational joint venture will involve the cooperative pooling of resources by the participants, and the sharing of the rewards of the joint venture. The multinational will therefore benefit from any business obtained or retained, or any permits, licenses, permissions or other advantages granted to the joint venture through improper payments to foreign officials.
2. **Local Content Requirement.** A joint venture with a local company may be a jurisdictional requirement to participate in that foreign government's tendering process. Many times a foreign public tender process will restrict

bidders to local companies or joint ventures that include a local company for content. The local company will likely use this requirement to negotiate an equal or majority equity interest and management control over the joint venture, adversely impacting the multinational's ability to control compliance.

3. **Joint Venture Partner Selection Process.** The foreign joint venture partner is usually selected based upon its knowledge of the local playing field and its connections to those players. Typically a business unit will attempt to nominate a strong local partner who is well connected within the country, with knowledge of how things are done to enhance the likelihood of business success. In many such situations, a company's law department will be brought into the discussions only after the preliminary negotiations have taken place, and perhaps even after the development of a term sheet, letter of intent or heads of agreement with the prospective partner. If compliance terms and conditions have not been a discussion in these preliminary negotiations, it may well be difficult to introduce them thereafter.

4. **The dreaded "Recommendation".** A governmental official may recommend the foreign joint venture partner. Unless the prospective partner was only one entity on a formal list of re-qualified local partners, such a recommendation should raise always red flag.

5. **Foreign Law Requirement.** It is often the case that when a foreign joint venture entity is formed, it is the local legal requirements that it must be formed under the laws of the foreign country. Such laws will usually dictate a certain

percentage equity interest by the foreign partner and the appointment of local personnel to officer and management positions.

6. **Locals Dealing with Locals.** The foreign joint venture partner often has the designated responsibility for day-to-day interface with local government officials. These joint venture representatives will blanch at the seconding of expensive US or Western European expatriates to the joint venture and may well thwart any such action if the foreign partner has an equal or controlling equity interest in the joint venture.

7. **Management Fee.** The foreign joint venture partner may receive a "management" fee, which may be used for improper purposes. Such fees may simply be based upon a percentage of joint venture revenue or profit, and often are not required to correspond to defined tasks, or specific efforts or hours. Typically there are no substantive billings associated with such fees, they simply become due. Under this type of arrangement, it is almost impossible to justify this fee if requested by the Department Of Justice.

8. **Books and Records.** The books and records of the joint venture, or portions of them, may be kept in the local language, complicating auditing. The problem becomes more difficult if the foreign joint venture partner is receiving the sponsor or management fees discussed above, and keeps its books of account only in the local language. Even if the books and records are maintained in English they usually are not kept up to a US public company, SOX or other standard. This in and of itself, is a violation of the FCPA.

9. **Can you talk the talk?** The multinational may not have financial oversight personnel with requisite language skills in the foreign country. Some companies have a policy that English will be used throughout the world in its business dealings. However, even with such an English only policy in place, the risks represented by such lack of effective oversight by the multinational extend not only to potential FCPA violations, but to other corrupt acts, including kickbacks, fraud and theft.

10. **Lack of Controls.** The joint venture may have local bank accounts or funds that do not require dual signatures, precluding a reasonable level of control over the use of joint venture funds. Once again, such a lack of controls may be a *per se* FCPA books and records violation.

Due Diligence

The starting point for any company is to engage in a due diligence investigation on any prospective foreign JV partners. Such a foreign entity or persons must provide enough basic information that a reasonable investigation can be performed. Haist breaks down his suggested due diligence inquires as follows:

1. Entity information
- Entity name, DBA, previous names, physical address and contact information, website address.
- Legal structure, jurisdiction of organization, date organized and whether the entity is publicly traded.

- Entity registration number(s), and dates and places of registration; number of years in business.
- Entity tax licenses, business licenses, or certificates or commercial registrations.
- Description of business, customers, industry sectors.
- Names, addresses and jurisdictions of formation for all companies or other affiliated entities, and ownership interest in each.
- Names and contact information for main point of contact.
- Names and contact information for entity's outside accountants/auditors and primary legal counsel.

2. Ownership information

- Name, address, nationality, percentage of ownership and date of acquisition for each parent company up to ultimate parent.
- Name, nationality, ID type/number, percent ownership and date of acquisition for all shareholders and owners (5 percent threshold more for publicly-listed entity).
- Identity of any other persons having a direct or indirect interest in the entity's equity, revenues or profits.
- Identity of any other person able to exercise control over the entity through any arrangement or relationship.
- Information on any direct or indirect ownership interest by any government, government employee or official; or political party, party official or candidate.

3. Management information

- Name, address, nationality, ID type/number and title for each member of the entity's governing board.
- Name, address, nationality, ID type/number and title for each officer of the entity.
- Information on any other business affiliations of principals, owners, partners, directors, officers or key employees who will manage the business relationship.
- Information on whether any principals, owners, partners, directors, officers or employees, currently or in the past, have been officials or candidates of a political party or been elected to any political office.

4. Government relationships

- Information on whether any principals, owners, partners, directors, officers or employees hold any official office or have any duties for any government agency or public international organization.
- Information on whether any owners, directors, officers or key employees have an immediate family member who is an employee, contractor or official of the foreign government, or a public international organization.
- Information on whether any employee of, or contractor or consultant to, any government entity or public international organization will benefit from the joint venture.
- Approximate percentage of entity's overall annual sales revenue derived from government sales.

5. Business conduct

- Information on whether the entity has ever been barred or suspended from doing business with a government entity Information on whether any principals, owners, partners, directors, officers or employees are identified on any government designated nationals, blocked persons, sanction, embargo or denied persons lists.
- Information on whether the entity, its principals, owners, partners, directors, officers or employees have ever been charged with, convicted of, or alleged to have been engaged in fraud, bribery, misrepresentation and/or any other criminal act.
- Information on whether the entity, its principals, owners, partners, directors, officers or employees have been investigated for violating the US Foreign Corrupt Practices Act or any anti-corruption law.
- Information on whether the entity has a compliance program which includes the prevention of bribery and information on the training of employees.

6. References

- Three or more unrelated business references, including a bank and existing client.

7. Certification/authorization/declaration

- Certification of accuracy.

- Authorization to conduct due diligence, authorization for third parties to release data and consent to collection of data.
- Anti-corruption compliance declaration.

Haist emphasized that an over-riding key is to document the entire process that your company goes through in investigated and creating a foreign JV. Additionally, it is important to remember, that obtaining this information is only one step. A company must evaluate the information and follow up if responses to such inquiries warrant such action. A paper program is simply not good enough and can lead to serious consequences if Red Flags are not reviewed and cleared.

Contract Issues

Haist believes that any JV Agreement with a Foreign Business Partner should include FCPA anti-bribery and corruption representations, warranties and covenants. Theses representations, warranties and covenants not to violate the FCPA should also include reference to the national and local anti-corruption laws of the foreign country, including laws enacted to comply with the OECD anti-bribery Convention and the UK Bribery Act. If the JV will operate in any other countries, the anti-corruption laws of those jurisdictions should be referenced as well.

Additional clauses that Haist suggests including in the JV Agreement are the following:

- A right of immediate termination for breach of the warranties or covenants relating to FCPA-anti-bribery and anti-corruption.
- A requirement for annual certification of compliance with such provisions by joint

venture partners and joint venture officers, managers and employees.

- Require that the joint venture follow generally accepted accounting principles (GAAP), and conduct an annual audit by an agreed upon independent accounting firm.
- The right to conduct ongoing audits of the joint venture books.
- Prohibit the creation of any funds without the approval of the joint venture's governing body (supermajority approval in the case of minority interest by the multinational).
- If the foreign joint venture partner has day-to-day management responsibilities, require dual signatures for checks or electronic funds transfers drawn on joint venture bank accounts.
- Require that the joint venture conduct investigative due diligence on agents, consultants and other third parties retained by the joint venture.
- Require the implementation of a code of business conduct by the joint venture and implement an anonymous reporting mechanism for joint venture employees.

Navigating the waters involving a foreign JV partner are tricky at best. In addition to all the business issues, the added requirements of the FCPA and the UK Bribery Act for foreign JV's make such a category of business relationship a potentially risky step. His article provides to the FCPA practitioner solid advice with which to provide counsel, whether you are in-house counsel or a lawyer in private practice, to your client who may be new to the foreign JV arena. Once again, we applaud him for putting together such an article to use as a guidepost when reviewing the creation of foreign JV, from an FCPA perspective.

8. Confidential Reporting and Internal Investigation

<u>Introduction</u>
This hallmark requires three separate components. The first is a confidential reporting system which is a mechanism for an organization's employees and others to report suspected or actual misconduct or violations of the company's policies on a confidential basis and without fear of retaliation. Second, after a credible allegation is made a company must have in place an efficient, reliable and properly funded process for investigating the allegation and documenting the company's response, including any disciplinary or remediation measures taken. Lastly, if there are any lessons to be learned from the results of the investigation, a company should update their internal controls and compliance program and focus future training on such issues, as appropriate.

What Are Some of the Benefits of a Compliance Hotline?

Posted August 12, 2012

Is your hotline working for you? The Securities and Exchange (SEC) Whistleblower line certainly appears to be working according to an article in the August issue of Compliance Week Magazine, entitled *"Promoting Effective Us of the Compliance Hotline"*, by Columnist José Tabuena. In the article, Tabuena quotes SEC Deputy Director of Enforcement George Canellos, who related at a recent conference that "What's really clear is quality of those tips has greatly improved and that market manipulation, dishonest accounting and potential violations of the Foreign Corrupt Practices Act (FCPA) are the most popular topics of whistleblower reports."

In his article Tabuena gave an excellent example of the power of a hotline. He wrote about the case study of a company which had not integrated its IT function into its regular compliance and ethics training programs. As such there were zero calls into the hotline by employees from the IT department. This dynamic was changed and IT was integrated into the company's regular compliance and ethics training. Thereafter, the hotline received several calls from IT department employees where there were two major areas of complaints. The first general area was that there were conflicts of interests between IT department managers, family members who were hired and perceptions of favoritism. The second generally revolved around allegations that certain company managers were manipulating data to maximize their bonuses.

The Favoritism Problem

The Human Resources (HR) department led an investigation that included questioning all IT managers about their direct reports and employees of their unit. The company determined that there was only one instance of a manger hiring a family member (a brother-in-law), but that person did not report to the manager and was in a different section of the IT organization. This finding made clear that there were misperceptions in the IT department, which affected the department morale. To remedy this all IT managers received training on appropriate employment practices, communications were also delivered to all IT employees explaining policies and practices regarding the hiring of family members. Most satisfyingly, Tabuena noted that during follow-up with callers to the helpline, the callers stated that the work environment in the IT department had noticeably improved. They also expressed gratitude that their questions were answered and that their issues were addressed. The callers felt their concerns were taken seriously when they saw the communications on hiring practices and upon having discussions with managers during staff meetings. Staff retention started improving in the department.

Manipulation of Data for Bonuses

The company used the hotline to obtain more information from the callers on "isolating the metrics and the managers in question." It was determined that the bonuses of a select few IT managers were indeed influenced by a questionable data source, which was controlled by a non-manager with minimal oversight and controls. Following interviews with the key individual and review of the data file (including forensic analysis), it was determined that one IT manager had misrepresented information provided to the staff person maintaining the data. Notably, this staff person also reported to this manager. As a result, the IT manager's bonus compensation was inflated. He was subsequently terminated.

Basic Tenets of an Effective Hotline

Tabuena provided three lessons which he felt were demonstrated in his article.

- First, a helpline is of no value if the workforce is not aware of it. Although a helpline was in place, it became apparent that a segment of the company had not been informed. It was hotline data that revealed this gap. By reviewing data segmented by region, department, incident classification, and other criteria, it became obvious in comparison to the rest of the organization that the IT department had not used the helpline.
- Second, the ethics and compliance office obtained support from the Chief Information Officer (CIO) for making IT part of the helpline community and for designating a liaison within the IT function. The support of department leadership likely influenced the success of the training and communications delivered by the ethics and compliance staff.
- Third, the awareness of the helpline is not sufficient to ensure success. The company made sure that issues and allegations were addressed and investigated, as needed. Employees who choose not to report wrongdoing indicate a belief that nothing will be done anyway, so why take the risk? Employees also cite fear of retaliation as a reason for not reporting.

Tabuena's article showed the power of a hotline. The company's Compliance Department "established the credibility of the helpline as a resource to raise issues and report misconduct. The concerns regarding nepotism and conflicts of interest were taken seriously, and although the violations were not as widespread as the calls indicated, the review went a long way to clear the air." Equally important, the helpline proved to be a successful management tool as well. The company was able to manage potential compliance issues and improve employee morale.

WHO Should Handle Serious Internal Investigation

Posted August 11, 2011

In the most recent issue of the Compliance and Ethics Professional Magazine, Issue 08/2011, is an article entitled *"Foxes and henhouses: The importance of independent counsel"*, in which author Dan Dunne discussed what he termed a "critical element" in any whistleblower response, which is a "fair and objective evaluation." Dunne wrote that a key component of this fair and objective evaluation is the WHO question; that is, who should supervise the investigation and who should handle the investigation? Dunne's clear conclusion is that independent counsel should handle any serious investigation.

Dunne list three factors which he believes should cause a company to retain independent counsel for internal investigations of serious whistleblower complaints. First, for any corporate ethics policy to be effective, it must be perceived to be fair. André Agassi was right, *perception is reality*. If your employees do not believe that the investigation is fair and impartial, then it is not fair and impartial. Further, those involved must have confidence that any internal investigation is treated seriously and objectively.

Secondly, if regular outside counsel investigates their own prior legal work or legal advice, Dunne believes that "a plethora of loyalty and privilege issues" can come up in the internal investigation. It is a rare legal investigation, where the lawyer or law firm which provided the legal advice and then investigates anything having to do with said legal advice, finds anything wrong with its legal advice. Dunne also notes that if the law firm which performs the internal investigation has to waive attorney client privilege, it may also have to do the same for all its legal work for the company.

The third point Dunne raises is the relationship of the regular outside counsel or law firm with regulatory authorities. If a company's regular outside counsel performs the internal investigation and the results turn out favorably for the company, the regulators may ask if the investigation was a "whitewash". If a regulatory authority, such as the Securities and Exchange Commission (SEC) or Department of Justice (DOJ) cannot rely on a company's own internal investigation, it may perform the investigation all over again with its own personnel. Further, these regulators may believe that the company, and its law firm, has engaged in a cover-up. This is certainly not the way to buy credibility.

Jim McGrath, writing in his Internal Investigations Blog, noted that despite the fact that using specialized investigation counsel is a best practice that is worth the money, one of the more difficult things is convincing decision-makers of this advantage. This is particularly so when speaking with mid- or small-sized companies that are part of larger supply chains. While general counsels and compliance officers may be up to speed on outsourcing critical inquiries, managers in business segments often are not and frequently reply that they've "got someone" in the company who "takes care of that stuff." However, it is clear that such an approach will be more costly to a company in the long run. McGrath emphasizes the need for independent counsel for serious corporate investigations.

I would add a couple more reasons to those listed by Dunne and McGrath. If there are serious allegations made concerning your company's employees engaging in criminal conduct, a serious response is required. Your company needs to hire some seriously good lawyers to handle any internal investigation. These lawyers need to have independence from the company so do not call your regular corporate counsel. Hire some seriously good investigative lawyers.

I believe that there is another reason to hire outside counsel. It is also important because, no matter what the outcome of your investigation, you will most probably have to deal with the government. If the investigation does reveal actionable conduct, your company will need legal counsel who is most probably an ex-DOJ prosecutor or ex-AUSA to get your company through that process. Even if there is a finding of no criminal activity, you will need very competent and very credible counsel to explain the investigation protocol and its results to the government.

One need only look at *L'Affair Renault* to see the hazards of not following the WHO approach of Dunne, McGrath or myself.

9. Continuous Improvement: Period Testing and Review

<u>Introduction</u>

As Lanny Breuer, the Assistant Attorney General for the Criminal Division of the US Department of Justice (DOJ) has stated on several occasions that I have heard him speak; a *best practices* compliance program should be evolving to meet the business and compliance changes which are constantly occurring across the globe. As a company's business changes over time, as do the environments in which it operates, the nature of its customers, the laws that govern its actions, and the standards of its industry. In addition, compliance programs that do not just exist on paper but are followed in practice will inevitably uncover compliance weaknesses and require enhancements. Therefore companies should regularly review and improve their compliance programs and not allow them to become stale.

Six Steps to Implementing Continuous Monitoring in your Compliance Program

Posted April 13, 2012

a) Anti-corruption, anti-bribery, anti-money laundering programs policies and procedures and even export control systems are seemingly in a constant state of evolution. Many companies are struggling with the challenge of implementing effective controls and monitoring risks across a spectrum that could include the three above listed compliance areas as well as others. One area which is evolving into a minimum best practices requirement for compliance is that of Continuous Monitoring (CM).

While many companies will look at CM as a software solution that can assist your company in managing risk; provide reporting metrics and, thereby, insights across an organization, it should be viewed more holistically. You will need to take many disparate systems, usually across a wide international geographic area, which may seem like an overwhelming process. However help is at hand from an article in the November 2011 issue of the Compliance Week Magazine, entitled *"Mission Impossible? Six steps to continuous monitoring"*, where author Justin Offen discusses his six-point program to ensure that your "CM solution doesn't become part of the problem" rather than a solution.

1. **Know your global IT footprint.** Offen believes that the challenges with integrating "disparate data often prevent CM discussions from even

getting off the ground." Rather it is important to understand how CM will be incorporated into your company's overall IT strategy as well as your compliance strategy. This advocates that this inquiry begins with understanding what your current IT structure is and what it is anticipated to be in 3 and 5 years. Once you identify your global IT footprint you can determine which system will be the best fit.

2. **Define scope and necessary resources.** The author believes that you need to determine what your goal is; begin by identifying your needs and then prioritize them. You should perform a risk analysis and then rank the risks. Here a risk ranking is not only helpful but can be critical to enable your company to focus on the needs specific of the organization. Regarding resources, you need to understand the amount of talent you have in your organization, identify who can implement and work with the system and determine your budget, which may need to be increased based upon your need for outside experts and unknown contingencies.

3. **Conduct a pilot or proof of concept.** Offen suggests that your company does not roll out an entire CM solution, company-wide, in one fell swoop but rather "business units and/or geographies should be prioritized and a phased in approach" utilized. This is one of the benefits of your risk analysis and risk ranking. This phased in approach can be used as a proof of concept, which the author believes "will yield greater operational efficiency throughout your CM solution implementation." Significantly it should enable you to chalk up an early success

to present to the inevitable nay-sayers in your organization.

4. **Decrease false positives.** Offen notes that it is "important to determine the effectiveness of each test prior to 'turning it on' in a CM solution." This is because improper or incomplete testing may well lead to a larger amount of false positives with which you are required to evaluate and clear. From each test, you can further refine your CM solution to the specific needs of your organization and increase time and efficiency in your overall CM program.

5. **Establish your escalation protocol.** The author believes that as part of your implementation, you should establish a response protocol when an exception or Red Flag arises. This protocol should include an escalation protocol if the Red Flag suggests that it is warranted or additional investigation determines a wider problem exists. This protocol should include specific individuals and departments that need to be notified, the makeup of your initial and secondary triage team and the accountability for each person in the process. A line should be set up for Board of Directors notification as well as a protocol to determine at what point to bring in outside counsel, if warranted.

6. **Demonstrate control through case management.** How does your company keep track of it all? I have long maintained that the three most important words in any compliance program are "document, document and document" but this must also include the caveat that you are able to produce the documentation, in a reasonable time, if a regulator requests.

Offen suggests that your company should be ready to "respond with appropriate documentation of any transaction that's been reviewed, showing the level of review and any additional steps taken."

The author has provided concrete steps which a compliance practitioner can take to implement or enhance a continuous monitoring system in an organization. He also points out the benefits to such a program, the creation of documentation which can lead to a 'ready response' by a company to an issue before it becomes a larger problem; coupled with the ability to recall all steps and information when a regulator comes knocking. Internally, using the pilots or proofs of concepts, the compliance department can bring in other stakeholders to see the value of continuous monitoring within the organization.

The Mercury 7, Chuck Duross and Continuous Improvement to Your Compliance Program

Posted February 15, 2012

Next Monday, February 20, 2012, is the 50th anniversary of the first American manned orbital space flight. It made John Glenn a national hero and heralded America's move into direct competition with the (then) Soviet Union for the race to put the first man on the moon. In an article in the New York Times (NYT), entitled *"At 90, John Glenn Looks Back"*, reporter John Noble Wilford wrote about this flight, the Mercury program, and Glenn based upon two interviews with the ex-astronaut and former Senator from Ohio. This coming Saturday, Glenn will be honored at Cape Canaveral at a celebration of the remaining members of the Mercury space team.

These original seven astronauts, known as the "Mercury 7", were true American heroes. Anyone who was interested in science in the slightest bit in the 60s knew who these men were. They were featured in Life Magazine with their families and each of their space flights were covered on live television by all three networks. Glenn is one of two of the Mercury 7 astronauts still alive, the other being Scott Carpenter who will also be honored on Saturday. The remaining members of the Mercury 7 astronauts were Deke Slayton, Gus Grissom, Alan Sheppard, Gordon Cooper and Wally Schirra. They were immortalized for a later generation by Tom Wolfe, in his book *"The Right Stuff"*.

So what is the compliance angle here? It is that NASA created an entire system, consisting of processes and procedures to put a man on the moon. Were there setbacks? Yes, the Apollo 1 tragedy still resonates at NASA today.

169

However NASA moved forward and fulfilled President Kennedy's vow to put a man on the moon by the end of the decade. NASA did this largely by continuous improvement of its system.

I thought about this article while reading the tweets coming from my *"This Week in FCPA"* co-host Howard Sklar last night. Howard is in Hong Kong, chairing the Anti-Corruption Asia Congress this week. Yesterday, Chuck Duross, Deputy Chief, Foreign Corrupt Practices Act (FCPA) Unit, United States Department of Justice (DOJ) spoke to the event and Howard tweeted some of the highlights of Chuck's remarks. They included:

- To combat anti-corruption, there needs to be political will, as it requires prosecution of bribe takers as well as bribe payers.
- Do not assume that your company is immune from FCPA liability just because you are not a US company. Here you should note that 9 out of the 10 FCPA settlements of all-time are with non-US based companies.
- Charging individuals leading to more trials. Last year the DOJ tried 3,000 cases last year and there were 4 FCPA trials. In Chuck's words, (as tweeted by Howard) *"Let's all take a breath"*.
- There was a FCPA trial first: a Foreign official, charged with money laundering, testified against the business bribe-payer. Here it is important to note that the DOJ can and will be charge foreign government offices.
- Turning to some specifics of compliance programs, Duross remarked that companies using half-measures to prevent bribery are at risk.

- Companies will receive a significant benefit for having robust compliance programs: lower fines, DPA/NPA, even not having a monitor. He gave some examples; Noble got an NPA, paid $2.6 MM, no monitor. Pride which sustained substantial cooperation with the DOJ, received below-the-guideline range penalty of 55%.
- Turning to the facilitation payment exception, Duross said that it is a narrow one: it's usually illegal locally where it is paid, discouraged in US, illegal internationally.
- He emphasized that third party agents need to be properly vetted.
- He noted that other violations of US law often accompany FCPA violations, such as anti-competitive behavior, trade violations, embezzlement, and money laundering.
- He emphasized that your company should do what it can do regarding your compliance program. If necessary, at first, change the tone at the top. Make it clear that illegal acts will not be tolerated. But you must mean it. Vocal support is necessary, but management's commitment cannot end there. Compliance is a cost center: management must back up vocal support of compliance with budget and resources.
- Next Duross suggested that companies reevaluate internal controls. They should take the time to review and test, think critically about risk.
- The DOJ looks at proactive compliance efforts when deciding how and whether to prosecute. He also suggested that your company might consider joining an integrity pact.

- Howard's tweets ended with this suggestion; that it is important to TEST your compliance program. You can run a fake invoice through your system which has information which should raise red flags. You can run information through the hotline and see what happens. That impresses the DOJ.

The last few points raised by Duross emphasized to me the process of compliance. But as important as putting the program in place is testing the program and using the lessons learned to upgrade and update your compliance program. While we celebrate John Glenn, the Mercury 7 and NASA for what they achieved, we should remember that NASA used continuous improvement in its space program. These same techniques can be brought to bear in your compliance program. Based upon the remarks of Chuck Duross, such monitoring, improvement and upgrades will be counted in a positive light by the DOJ if you are involved in a FCPA enforcement action.

How do You Evaluate a Risk Assessment?

Posted September 16, 2011

What is the amount of risk that your company is willing to accept? Before you even get to this question how does your company assess risk and subsequently evaluate that risk? In the July issue of the Compliance Week magazine, these questions were explored in an article entitled *"Improving Risk Assessments and Audit Operations"* in which author Tammy Whitehouse discussed the audit process and how the audit results can form the basis for the evaluation of a risk assessment. In her article Whitehouse focused on the presentation of Michele Abraham, from Timken Co., and how Timken assesses and then monitors risks it determines through its annual compliance audit.

According to Abraham, once risks are identified, they are then rated according to their significance and likelihood of occurring, and then plotted on a heat map to determine their priority. The most significant risks with the greatest likelihood of occurring are deemed the priority risks, which become the focus of the audit monitoring plan, she said. A variety of solutions and tools can be used to manage these risks going forward but the key step is to evaluate and rate these risks. Abraham provided two examples of ratings guides which Whitehouse included in her article. We quote both in their entirety.

LIKELIHOOD

Likelihood Rating	Assessment	Evaluation Criteria
1	Almost Certain	High likely, this event is expected to occur

2	Likely	Strong possibility that an event will occur and there is sufficient historical incidence to support it
3	Possible	Event may occur at some point, typically there is a history to support it
4	Unlikely	Not expected but there's a slight possibility that it may occur
5	Rare	Highly unlikely, but may occur in unique circumstances

'Likelihood' factors to consider: The existence of controls, written policies and procedures designed to mitigate risk capable of leadership to recognize and prevent a compliance breakdown; Compliance failures or near misses; Training and awareness programs.

PRIORITY

Priority Rating	Assessment	Evaluation Criteria
1-2	Severe	Immediate action is required to address the risk, in addition to inclusion in training and education and audit and monitoring plans
3-4	High	Should be proactively monitored and mitigated through inclusion in training and education and audit and monitoring plans
5-7	Significant	
8-14	Moderate	
15-19	Low	Risks at this level should be monitored but do not necessarily pose any serious threat to the organization at the present time.
20-25	Trivial	

Priority Rating: Product of 'likelihood' and significance ratings reflects the significance of particular risk universe. It is not a measure of compliance effectiveness or to compare efforts, controls or programs against peer groups.

At Timken, the most significant risks with the greatest likelihood of occurring are deemed to be the priority risks. These "Severe" risks become the focus of the audit monitoring plan going forward. A variety of tools can be used, such as continuous controls monitoring with tools like those provided by Visual Risk IQ, a relationship-analysis based software such as Catelas or other analytical based tools. But you should not forget the human factor. At Timken, one of the methods used by the compliance group to manage such risk is by providing employees with substantive training to guard against the most significant risks coming to pass and to keep the key messages fresh and on everyone's mind. The company also produces a risk control summary that succinctly documents the nature of the risk and the actions taken to mitigate it.

The key to the Timken approach is the action steps prescribed by their analysis. This is another way of saying that the risk assessment *informs* the compliance program, not vice versa. This is the method set forth by the US Department of Justice (DOJ) in its Compliance Program *best practices* and in the UK Bribery Act's *Adequate Procedures*. I believe that the DOJ wants to see a reasoned approach with regards to the actions a company takes in the compliance arena. The model set forth by Michele Abraham of Timken certainly is a reasoned approach and can provide the articulation needed to explain which steps were taken.

10. Mergers and Acquisition

Introduction

In the context of the Foreign Corrupt Practices Act (FCPA), mergers and acquisitions (M&A) present both risks and opportunities. A company that does not perform adequate FCPA due diligence prior to a merger or acquisition may face both legal and business risks, including most commonly under the FCPA that inadequate due diligence can allow a course of bribery to continue - with all the attendant harms to a business's profitability and reputation, as well as potential civil and criminal liability. However pre-acquisition due diligence is only a part of the picture required under this prong. The FCPA also mandates that an acquiring company should, within a reasonable time frame promptly incorporate the acquired company into all of its internal controls, including its compliance program. Companies should consider training new employees, reevaluating third parties under company standards, and, where appropriate, conducting audits on new business units.

The DOJ Listens: the Evolution of FCPA Compliance in M&A

Posted June 21, 2012

Earlier this week the US Department of Justice (DOJ) released a Deferred Prosecution Agreement (DPA) with the company Data Systems & Solutions LLC (DS&S). I explored the factual allegations against DS&S and the highlights of the DPA in yesterday's post. Today I want to discuss the DS&S DPA in the context of the DOJ's evolution in thinking regarding what a company can do to protect itself under the Foreign Corrupt Practices Act (FCPA) when it purchases another entity or otherwise engages in mergers and acquisitions (M&A) work. In other words, forces the evolution of *best practices*.

Previously many compliance practitioners had based decisions in the M&A context on DOJ Opinion Release 08-02 (08-02), which related to Halliburton's proposed acquisition of the UK entity, Expro. In the spring of 2011, the Johnson & Johnson (J&J) DPA changed the perception of compliance practitioners regarding what is required of a company in the M&A setting related to FCPA due diligence, both pre and post-acquisition. On June 18, the DOJ released the DS&S DPA which brought additional information to the compliance practitioner on what a company can do to protect itself in the context of M&A activity.

Opinion Release 08-02 began as a request from Halliburton to the DOJ from issues that arose in the pre-acquisition due diligence of the target company Expro. Halliburton had submitted a request to the DOJ specifically posing these three questions: (1) whether the proposed acquisition transaction itself would violate the FCPA; (2) whether, through the proposed acquisition of Target, Halliburton would "inherit" any FCPA liabilities of Target for pre-acquisition unlawful conduct; and (3) whether Halliburton would be held criminally liable for any post-acquisition unlawful conduct by Target prior to Halliburton's completion of its FCPA and anti-corruption due diligence, where such conduct is identified and disclosed to the Department within 180 days of closing.

I. *08-02 Conditions*

Halliburton committed to the following conditions, if it was the successful bidder in the acquisition:

1. **Within ten business days of the closing.** Halliburton would present to the DOJ a comprehensive, risk-based FCPA and anti-corruption due diligence work plan which would address, among other things, the use of agents and other third parties; commercial dealings with state-owned customers; any joint venture, teaming or consortium arrangements; customs and immigration matters; tax matters; and any government licenses and permits. The Halliburton work plan committed to organizing the due diligence effort into *high risk*, *medium risk*, and *lowest risk* elements.
   a) **Within 90 days of Closing.** Halliburton would report to the DOJ the results of its high risk due diligence.
   b) **Within 120 days of Closing.** Halliburton would report to the DOJ the results to date of its medium risk due diligence.
   c) **Within 180 days of Closing.** Halliburton would report to the DOJ the

results to date of its lowest risk due diligence.

d) **Within One Year of Closing.** Halliburton committed full remediation of any issues which it discovered within one year of the closing of the transaction.

Many lawyers were heard to exclaim, "What an order, we cannot go through with it." However, we advised our clients not to be discouraged because 08-02 laid out a clear road map for dealing with some of the difficulties inherent in conducting sufficient pre-acquisition due diligence in the FCPA context. Indeed the DOJ concluded 08-02 by noting, "Assuming that Halliburton, in the judgment of the Department, satisfactorily implements the post-closing plan and remediation detailed above... the Department does not presently intend to take any enforcement action against Halliburton."

II. *Johnson & Johnson "Enhanced Compliance Obligations"*

Attachment D of the J&J DPA, entitled "Enhanced Compliance Obligations", is a list of compliance obligations in which J&J agreed to undertake certain enhanced compliance obligations for at least the duration of its DPA beyond the minimum *best practices* also set out in the J&J DPA. With regard to the M&A context, J&J agreed to the following:

7. J&J will ensure that new business entities are only acquired after thorough FCPA and anti-corruption due diligence by legal, accounting, and compliance personnel. Where such anti-corruption due diligence is not practicable prior

to acquisition of a new business for reasons beyond J&J's control, or due to any applicable law, rule, or regulation, J&J will conduct FCPA and anti-corruption due diligence subsequent to the acquisition and report to the Department any corrupt payments, falsified books and records, or inadequate internal controls as required by … the Deferred Prosecution Agreement.

8. J&J will ensure that J&J's policies and procedures regarding the anti-corruption laws and regulations apply as quickly as is practicable, but in any event no less than one year post-closing, to newly-acquired businesses, and will promptly, for those operating companies that are determined not to pose corruption risk, J&J will conduct periodic FCPA Audits, or will incorporate FCPA components into financial audits.

   a. Train directors, officers, employees, agents, consultants, representatives, distributors, joint venture partners, and relevant employees thereof, who present corruption risk to J&J, on the anticorruption laws and regulations and J&J's related policies and procedures; and

   b. Conduct an FCPA-specific audit of all newly-acquired businesses within 18 months of acquisition.

These enhanced obligations agreed to by J&J in the M&A context were less time sensitive than those agreed to by Halliburton in 08-02. In the J&J DPA, the company agreed to following time frames:

A. **18 Month** - conduct a full FCPA audit of the acquired company.

B. **12 Month** - introduce full anti-corruption compliance policies and procedures into the acquired company and train those persons and business representatives which "present corruption risk to J&J."

So there is no longer a risk based approach as set out in 08-02 and the tight time frames are also relaxed. Once again we applaud the DOJ for setting out specific information for the compliance practitioner through the release of the J&J DPA. As many have decried 08-02 is a standard too difficult to satisfy in the real world of time constraints and budget cuts, the "Acquisition" component of the J&J DPA should provide those who have made this claim with some relief.

III. DS&S

In the DS&S DPA there are two new items listed in the Corporate Compliance Program, attached as Schedule C to the DPA, rather than the standard 13 items we have seen in every DPA since at least November 2010. The new additions are found on items 13 & 14 on page C-6 of Schedule C and deal with mergers and acquisitions. They read in full:

> *13. DS&S will develop and implement policies and procedures for mergers and acquisitions requiring that DS&S conduct appropriate risk-based due diligence on potential new business entities, including appropriate FCPA and anti-corruption due diligence by legal, accounting, and compliance personnel. If DS&S discovers*

> *any corrupt payments or inadequate internal controls as part of its due diligence of newly acquired entities or entities merged with DS&S, it shall report such conduct to the Department as required in Appendix B of this Agreement.*
>
> *14. DS&S will ensure that DS&S's policies and procedures regarding the anticorruption laws apply as quickly as is practicable to newly acquired businesses or entities merged with DS&S and will promptly:*
>
>> *a. Train directors, officers, employees, agents, consultants, representatives, distributors, joint venture partners, and relevant employees thereof, who present corruption risk to DS&S, on the anti-corruption laws and DS&S's policies and procedures regarding anticorruption laws.*
>>
>> *b. Conduct an FCPA-specific audit of all newly acquired or merged businesses as quickly as practicable.*

This language draws from and builds upon the prior Opinion Release 08-02 regarding Halliburton's request for guidance and the J&J Enhanced Compliance Obligations incorporated into its DPA. While the DS&S DPA does note that it is specifically tailored as a solution to DS&S's FCPA compliance issues, I believe that this is the type of guidance that a compliance practitioner can rely upon when advising his or her clients on what the DOJ expects during M&A activities.

FCPA M&A Box Score Summary

Time Frames	Halliburton 08-02	J&J	DS&S
FCPA Audit	1. High Risk Agents - **90 days** 2. Medium Risk Agents - **120 Days** 3. Low Risk Agents - **180 days**	**18 months** to conduct full FCPA audit	As soon *"as practicable"*
Implement FCPA Compliance Program	Immediately upon closing	**12 months**	As soon *"as practicable"*
Training on FCPA Compliance Program	**60 days** to complete training for high risk employees, **90 days** for all others	**12 months** to complete training	As soon *"as practicable"*

I believe that the DOJ does listen to the concerns of US companies about issues relating to FCPA enforcement, which is consistent with its duty to uphold that law. Last month we saw the issue of the Morgan Stanley declination in the context of the Garth Peterson FCPA prosecution. With the DS&S DPA, there is clearly more flexible language presented in the context of M&A work and potential liability for 'buying a FCPA claim.'

How to Create a Post-Acquisition FCPA Compliance Program Integration Plan

Posted December 11, 2012

Your company has just made its largest acquisition ever and your Chief Executive Officer (CEO) says that he wants you to have a compliance post-acquisition integration plan on his desk in one week. Where do you begin? Of course you think about the recently released Department of Justice (DOJ) Guidance on the Foreign Corrupt Practices Act (FCPA) but remember that it did not have the time lines established in the recent enforcement actions involving Johnson & Johnson (J&J), Pfizer and Defendant Data Systems & Solutions LLC (DS&S) regarding post-acquisition integration of a FCPA compliance program by an acquiring company into a company. While there are time frames listed in the Deferred Prosecution Agreements (DPAs) that can be ascertained, one of the things that most compliance professionals struggle with is how to perform these post-acquisition compliance integrations. I recently saw an article in the December issue of the Harvard Business Review, entitled *"Two Routes to Resilience"*, which presented some concepts that I thought might be of use to the compliance practitioner in a post-acquisition compliance program integration scenario. It certainly might give you some ideas to present to your CEO next week.

The authors, Clark Gilbert, Matthew Eyring and Richard Foster reviewed the situation where an entity must transform itself in response to various factors such as market shifts, new technologies or low cost start-ups providing competition. In order to make such a transition, the authors posit that two transformations must take place. The first one "adapts the core business to the realities of the disrupted marketplace." This process creates a "disruptive business" within the older more established culture. This leads to the second transformation, which the authors denominate as "establishing a 'capabilities exchange'- a new organizational process that allows the two efforts to share resources without interfering with each other's operations." It is this second transformation that I want to focus on in this article.

Anyone who has gone through a large merger or acquisition knows how terrifying it can be for the individual employee. Many people, particularly at the acquired company, will be fearful of losing their jobs. This fear, mis-placed or well-founded, can lead to many difficulties in the integration process. In whatever time frame the FCPA compliance practitioner faces: whether 18 months under the J&J DPA, 12 months under the Pfizer DPA or 'as soon as is practicable' under the language of the DS&S DPA; the process needs to move forward in an expeditious manner. In their article, the authors suggest the creation of a 'Capabilities Exchange' which allows "the two organizations to live together and share strengths" and will coordinate "the two transformational efforts so that each gets what it needs and is protected from [unwanted] interference by the other." The authors put forth five steps in this process.

1. **Establish Leadership.** The authors note that while this may be the "simplest step but also the one most open to abuse." The authors believe that the process should be run by just a few top people. To establish the correct 'tone-at-the-top' I believe that you will need the CEO, Chief Financial Officer (CFO) and Chief Compliance Officer (CCO) of the acquiring company and a similar counter-part from the acquired company.

2. **Identify the resources the two organizations can or need to share.** Here the authors are concerned with how much can be brought from the acquired organization into the integration. Hopefully the acquiring organization will have some idea of the state of the compliance program before the deal is closed. It may be that there is some or all of a minimum *best practices* compliance program in place. If so, attention needs to turn to what can continue and how will need to be integrated.
3. **Create Exchange Teams.** The authors recognize that in many "synergy efforts, everyone is expected to think about ways resources might be shared." However, they advocated that in Capability Exchanges, the responsibility should be "carefully confined to a series of teams." Senior leadership should create these teams by assigning a small number of people from both entities with the responsibility of allocating resources used in the integration project.
4. **Protect Boundaries.** The authors believe that for true transformation to take place the organization "must operate as if the future of the company depended on it." But they must do so in a way that does not "stomp on the camel's nose" simply because it sticks it in the tent. Once again the Leadership Team established under Item 1 must provide back up if policing boundaries is needed.
5. **Scale up and promote the new compliance program.** Interestingly the authors believe that it is important to celebrate and promote the new entity to both the acquiring company, others in the company and even external stakeholders. It

is important that markets and others in the same or similar industry see this evolution and growth.

Given the pressures and time frames in both the pre-and post-acquisition arenas, I believe this article provides some insight into how the CCO or compliance practitioner can think about the compliance program integration that is required in the mergers and acquisition (M&A) context. While the ideas presented by the authors relate to a different area, I believe that they can provide insight into the compliance field as well. It also could of great use to you in presenting a program to your CEO.

Part II - THE UK BRIBERY ACT

A. The Six Principles of Adequate Procedures Compliance Regime

Principle I - Proportionate Procedures: Bonnie Prince Charlie, Charlie Chaplin and Proportionate Procedures

Posted April 17, 2012

Today, we note a birthday anniversary and the anniversary of an event involving two quite different Charlie's. The first is the anniversary of the Battle of Culloden, where in 1746 the English forces, led by the Duke of Cumberland, defeated the Scottish Jacobites, who supported the last serious Stuart Pretender to the English throne, Bonnie Prince Charlie. This battle not only cemented the House of Hanover's seat on the English throne but also led to the decimation of the Scottish Highland Clans. In a very different anniversary celebration, we also note the birthday of Charlie Chaplin, born in 1889. Yes, the Little Tramp was a Brit.

Whilst flying over to the UK I caught up on some reading, including the Saturday Wall Street Journal (WSJ). In an article, entitled *"Why Airport Security is Broken-And How to Fix It"*, Kip Hawley, the former head of the US Transport Security Administration (TSA) provides his prescription on how to fix what he calls "the national embarrassment that our airport security remains". Pretty strong language by someone who has been "to the top of the mountain." While I find the security checks we all now go through only mildly inconveniencing, Hawley writes that the US airport security remains "hopelessly bureaucratic and disconnected from the people whom it is meant to protect."

Hawley believes that the TSA has an incorrect approach to proportionality of the risk faced. He says that by attempting to eliminate all risk, the system is not only a "nightmare for U.S. and visitors from overseas" but that this system is "brittle where it needs to be supple." In the aftermath of the post 9-11 attacks the system was designed so every passenger could avoid harm while traveling. Hawley believes that some of the risk factors which led to the 9-11 attacks have been remedied, such as box cutters or small knives that could breach a cockpit door; more Federal Air Marshalls traveling on flights and greater passenger awareness and willingness to respond to such an emergency. He believes that the risk, which is now paramount, to manage is to stop a catastrophic attack. In short the risks have changed but the TSA have not changed to manage new or other risks.

Hawley lays out five changes which he believes would go a long way towards allowing the TSA to properly manage this risk of catastrophic attack:

1. **No more banned items.** By listing every banned item, you make each X-Ray scan an "Easter-egg hunt" and provide terrorists with the list of items the TSA will look for.
2. **Allow all liquids.** Hawley believes that "simple checkpoint signage, a small software update and some traffic management are all that are standing between you and bringing all your liquids on a plane. Really."
3. **Give TSA officers more flexibility and rewards for initiative and hold them accountable.** There must be more independence for TSA officers 'on the ground.' Currently if you initiate independence as a TSA officer, you are more likely to be disciplined rather than rewarded.

4. **Eliminate baggage fees.** The airlines bags fees cause more passengers to bring bags on planes, which requires more security, increases costs and slows down the process which in turn requires airlines to charge more for tickets because there are more delays.
5. **Randomize security.** If terrorists know what to expect at airport security, they have a greater chance to evade the system. Hawley's answer is to randomize more security checks while not subjecting every passenger to the current full security compliment.

I have set out Hawley's thoughts in some detail because they point to how the UK Ministry of Justice (MOJ) suggests that a company should begin its anti-bribery/anti-corruption compliance program. It discusses what constitutes the Six Principles of Adequate Procedures compliance program in Principle 1, entitled Proportionate Procedures, the MOJ Guidance states, *"A commercial organisation's procedures to prevent bribery by persons associated with it are proportionate to the bribery risks it faces and to the nature, scale and complexity of the commercial organisation's activities."* In other words, adequate anti-bribery prevention procedures should be proportionate to the bribery risks that a company faces. It all begins with a risk assessment, but the Guidance recognizes that *"To a certain extent the level of risk will be linked to the size of the organisation and the nature and complexity of its business."* However, company size is not to be the only determining factor as certainly smaller entities may face quite significant risks and, therefore, need more extensive procedures than their counterparts facing limited risks. The Guidance does recognize that the majority of small organizations are unlikely to need procedures that are as extensive as those of a large multi-national organization.

The level of risk that a business may face will also vary with the type and nature of the persons with which it is has third party relationships. A company that properly assesses that it has no risk of bribery on the part of one of its third party relationships will accordingly require nothing in the way of procedures to prevent bribery in the context of that relationship. By the same token the bribery risks associated with reliance on a third party agent representing a company in negotiations with foreign public officials may be assessed as significant and accordingly require much more in the way of procedures to mitigate those risks. This means that companies will be required to select procedures to cover a broad range of risks but any consideration by a "court in an individual case of the adequacy of procedures is likely necessarily to focus on those procedures designed to prevent bribery on the part of the associated person committing the offence in question."

Near the end of this section of the Guidance it states, *"the procedures should seek to ensure there is a practical and realistic means of achieving the organisation's stated anti-bribery policy objectives across all of the organisation's functions."* This sounds quite similar to Hawley's plea that the TSA needs to change its risk management away from protecting every passenger from harm while traveling to preventing a catastrophic attack. But perhaps this final point from the Guidance points up to why the TSA cannot or will not make this change in risk management. They have not received firm guidance from the Executive Branch or from US Congress on what their primary mission is, and hence the primary risk the TSA must manage. In other words, if top management does not support the Compliance Department or forces it to focus on the wrong risks, a

Compliance Department may well miss the mark and cause its clients, the business unit personnel to become fed up and just as irritated with the Compliance Department as Hawley believes the traveling public is with the TSA. In other words, tone at the top does matter. Not only must senior management support the compliance function but it should support it, with the appropriate financial resources and tools to manage the correct risks.

Principle II - Top Level Commitment: Monty Python, the Holy Grail & Principle II of Adequate Procedures

Posted April 20, 2012

I have long wondered why was it that the Knights of the Roundtable were searching for the Holy Grail? I mean, what would a chalice, first used in the Last Supper and then used to drain the blood of Jesus after crucifixion, being doing in Britain? The story is a bit convoluted but this is what I have learned this week; that is it is a part of the legend of King Arthur and it goes something like this.

Joseph of Arimathea, the man who brought down the body of Jesus from the cross after he was crucified, later brought the Holy Grail to Britain with him when he became the first Christian Bishop of Britain. It was hidden and could only be found by a righteous Knight, who turned out to be Sir Perceval. What I did not know was the Sir Perceval was actually the son of Sir Lancelot from a witch, who came to Sir Lancelot in the form of Lady Guinevere, who, nine months later, gave birth to a boy who later became the Knight Sir Perceval.

As I said, all quite confusing as there are apparently variations upon variations of this myth. I think I will just stick with Monty Python and their Holy Grail version. At least we know how to answer the three questions to safely cross the Bridge of Death: (1) What is your name? (fill in the blank); (2) What is your quest? (I seek the Holy Grail.); and (3) What is the air-speed velocity of an unladen swallow?

All of this brings me to the UK Bribery Act and the Six Principles of Adequate Procedures compliance program and today's topic, Principle II - Top-level Commitment. The purpose of Principle II is to encourage the involvement of top-level management in the determination of bribery prevention procedures. Under Principle II the top-level management of a business, whether a board of directors, the owners or any other equivalent body or person, must be committed to preventing bribery by persons associated with it. This top-level of management should foster a culture within the company in which bribery is never acceptable. The UK Ministry of Justice (MOJ) Guidance comments that those persons who are at the top of a business "are in the best position to foster a culture of integrity where bribery is unacceptable." The Guidance provides that top-level management commitment to bribery prevention is likely to include (1) communication of a company's anti-bribery stance, and (2) an appropriate degree of top-level involvement in developing bribery prevention procedures.

I.   *Internal and external communication of the commitment to zero tolerance of bribery*

The Guidance lists several steps that a company can take to establish this tone of top-level commitment to zero tolerance of bribery. There could be a formal written statement communicating this commitment to establish an anti-bribery culture within an organization. The Guidance recognizes that there could be several forms of communication, which might be tailored to different audiences within the company and could be generally available, for example on a company's intranet and internet site. This commitment should be emphasized so as to draw employees' attention on a periodic basis to this commitment.

The Guidance provides some touchstones regarding the types of concepts that a formal statement should include to demonstrate that the top-level commitment is viewed as effective:

- A commitment to carry out business fairly, honestly and openly, with transparency;
- A commitment to zero tolerance towards bribery and corruption;
- The negative consequences of breaching the policy for employees and managers; to those business partners the company might engage, explaining the consequences of breaching contractual provisions relating to anti-bribery and anti-corruption prevention;
- A statement of the positive benefits for both the company and its employees of the business benefits of rejecting bribery. This would include the reputation of the company with customers and the confidence of its business partners and the incentives for employees to do business in such a compliant manner;
- There should be a reference to the range of anti-bribery prevention procedures the company has or is putting in place, including any protection and procedures for confidential reporting of bribery such as anonymous reporting through a helpline or hotline;
- A clear communication that key company individuals and departments are involved in the development and implementation of the company's anti-bribery and anti-corruption prevention procedures; and
- Reference to the company's public facing involvement in any collective action against

bribery and corruption in its same business sector.

II.   *Top-level involvement in bribery prevention*

The Guidance intones that effective leadership in bribery prevention will take a variety of forms appropriate for and proportionate to a company's "size, management structure and circumstances." In smaller companies this could mean that top-level managers be personally involved in initiating, developing and implementing anti-bribery and anti-corruption prevention procedures and critical decision making. Conversely, in a large multi-national, the Board of Directors should be responsible for setting bribery prevention policies, tasking management to design, operate and monitor bribery prevention procedures, and keeping these policies and procedures under regular review. The Guidance sets forth several elements which it believes are symptomatic of top-level engagement in a company's anti-bribery and anti-corruption compliance effort. They include:

- There should be top-level involvement in the selection and training of senior managers to lead anti-bribery work where appropriate;
- Top-level leadership on key measures such as a code of conduct;
- There should be top-level endorsement of all bribery prevention related publications;
- Top-level management should lead the company in awareness raising and encouraging transparent dialogue to ensure effective dissemination of anti-bribery and anti-corruption policies and procedures to employees;

- Top-level management should be engaged or involved in oversight of appropriate third party business partners;
- Top management should demonstrate leadership through relevant external bodies, such as industry trade groups or other similar organizations and the media, to help articulate both the company's overall compliance efforts and industry commitment in the fight against bribery and corruption;
- There should be specific top-level involvement in high profile and critical decision making where appropriate;
- Top-level management must assure that not only an appropriate risk assessment is conducted but that it informs the company's anti-bribery and anti-corruption compliance program and not the other way around; and
- Top-level management should have general oversight of breaches of procedures and the provision of feedback to the company's Board of Directors or equivalent, where appropriate, on levels of compliance.

The MOJ Guidance once again provides solid detail on the elements which should go into your anti-bribery and anti-corruption compliance program. It also provides the basis for several different metrics that you can set up to measure how well top-level management is involved and engaged in your compliance regime.

As to the answer to the final question from Monty Python, it depends, *"What do you mean? An African or European swallow?*

Principle III - Risk Assessments: Risk Assessments under the UK Bribery Act

Posted February 28, 2012

In the February 10, 2012 edition of the Houston Business Journal, in an article entitled *"In order to solve a problem, it must first be identified"*, author Harvey Mackay wrote "People don't usually buy products and services. They buy solutions to problems." He notes that successful sales people "tailor their products and services to meet a demand". However, in compliance the 'demand' that often needs to be satisfied is risk. In your role as a compliance professional, you need to be able to identify risk and then design a system to manage it. If you review a proposed transaction and concluded it would violate the Foreign Corrupt Practices Act (FCA) and then reported that to senior management, you may well be told that it is the job of compliance to manage compliance risks, now go back and figure out a way to manage that risk so that the transaction can be done within the law. The question is how to determine the compliance risk so that it can be managed. The answer is by performing a risk assessment.

In three enforcement actions in early 2011, the Department of Justice (DOJ) indicated FCPA compliance risk areas which should be evaluated for a minimum *best practices* FCPA compliance program. Both the Alcatel-Lucent and Maxwell Technologies Deferred Prosecution Agreements (DPAs) listed the following seven areas of risk to be assessed.

1. Geography - Where does your Company do business?

2. Interaction with types and levels of Governments.
3. Industrial Sector of Operations.
4. Involvement with Joint Ventures.
5. Licenses and Permits in Operations.
6. Degree of Government Oversight.
7. Volume and Importance of Goods and Personnel Going Through Customs and Immigration.

However, the British government has gone further in providing guidance around the parameters of a risk assessment. The UK Ministry of Justice (MOJ), in Principle III of the Six Principles of Adequate Procedures compliance program, discusses risk assessment. It mandates that a company should assess "the nature and extent of its exposure to potential external and internal risks of bribery on its behalf by persons associated with it." Further a risk assessment should be performed on a periodic basis, it should be reasoned and it should be documented. From this risk assessment, a company should then be able to "promote the adoption of risk assessment procedures that are proportionate to the organisation's size and structure and to the nature, scale and location of its activities."

The MOJ has collected the risks which should be assessed into five broad groups and they are country, business sector, transaction, business opportunity and business partnership:

1. *Country risk*. This is evidenced by perceived high levels of corruption, an absence of effectively implemented anti-bribery legislation and a failure of the foreign government, media, local business community and civil society

effectively to promote transparent procurement and investment policies.

2. ***Sector risk.*** Some sectors are higher risk than others. Higher risk sectors include the extractive industries and the large scale infrastructure sector.

3. ***Transaction risk.*** Certain types of transaction give rise to higher risks, for example, charitable or political contributions, licenses and permits, and transactions relating to public procurement.

4. ***Business opportunity risk.*** These risks might arise in high value projects or with projects involving many contractors or intermediaries; or with projects which are not apparently undertaken at market prices, or which do not have a clear legitimate objective.

5. ***Business partnership risk.*** There are some relationships which involve higher risk, for example, the use of intermediaries in transactions with foreign public officials; consortia or joint venture partners; and relationships with politically exposed persons where the proposed business relationship involves, or is linked to, a prominent public official.

Additionally, the MOJ believes that the areas of risk that are assessed should enable a company to accurately identify and prioritize the risks it faces, whatever its size, activities, customers or markets, as these usually reflect a few basic characteristics. They listed these as:

- Oversight of the risk assessment by top level management. More than simply tone at the top but is management truly committed to installing and maintaining a culture of compliance?

- Appropriate resourcing – this should reflect the scale of the organization's business and the need to identify and prioritize all relevant risks. Have your designated persons with authority to make compliance decisions and back that up with the budget required to do so.
- Identification of the internal and external information sources that will enable risk to be assessed and reviewed. Who are you are going to use for the risk assessment?
- Due diligence enquiries. Is your due diligence sufficient, if not, what are you going to do to resolve this issue?
- Accurate and appropriate documentation of the risk assessment and its conclusions. Document, Document, Document.

So the key is to assess the risk. From both the DOJ and MOJ, there is specific guidance of the quality of risks that should be assessed. A risk assessment is a key tool to use to identify the types of problems that the compliance group needs to solve, or at least manage. A risk assessment should not be an annual exercise that your company goes through. You can use the guidance from the DOJ or MOJ in a wide variety of circumstances, down to the granular transactional level. Or as Harvey Mackay might say, to solve a problem, you first need to identify that problem.

Principle IV - Due Diligence: Henry IV

Posted April 24, 2012

As a father, I have come to appreciate Shakespeare's *Henry IV* more and more; particularly more than I did when I was only a son. Part of the play deals with how Henry IV got his crown, by deposing Richard II and the battles he had to fight to keep it. But a large part of the play deals with his riotous son, Hal, drinking and philandering with Falstaff before he grew into the great monarch *Henry V*. With that in mind, we continue our exploration of the Six Principles of Adequate Procedures compliance defense with a look at Principle IV - Due Diligence.

I.   Commentary

Principle IV of the Six Principles of Adequate Procedures compliance program states, *"The commercial organisation applies due diligence procedures, taking a proportionate and risk based approach, in respect of persons who perform or will perform services for or on behalf of the organisation, in order to mitigate identified bribery risks."* The purpose of Principle IV is to encourage businesses to put in place due diligence procedures that adequately inform the application of proportionate measures designed to prevent persons associated with a company, whether on the sales and distribution side or in the supply chain, from bribing on their behalf. The Guidance recognizes that due diligence procedures act both as a procedure for anti-bribery risk assessment and as a risk mitigation technique. The Guidance believes that due diligence is so important that "the role of due diligence in bribery risk mitigation justifies its inclusion here as a Principle in its own right."

II.   Who is an Associated Person?

Who is an Associated Person? The Guidance intones that a company is liable if a person 'associated' with it bribes another person intending to obtain, retain or a gain an advantage for the business. The definition is quite broad and is applicable to basically anyone who 'performs services' for or on behalf of the business. This can be an individual, an incorporated entity or unincorporated body. The capacity in which the services are provided is not dispositive, so employees, agents and subsidiaries are included. This also means that a supplier can properly be said to be performing services for a company rather than simply acting as the seller of goods, it may also be an 'associated' person. Taken further, if a supply chain involves several entities, or a project is to be performed by a prime contractor with a series of sub-contractors, a business is likely to only exercise control over its relationship with its contractual counterpart and this means a company could have responsibility for those acting on its behalf in a wide range of arenas, with a wide range of titles. This could include all of the following: agent, sales agent, reseller, distributor, partner, joint ventures (JV), consortium partner, contractor, subcontractor, vendor, supplier, affiliate, subsidiary or any other similar moniker.

III.   Joint Ventures

As for JV, these come in many different forms, sometimes operating through a separate legal entity, but at other times through contractual arrangements. In the case of a JV operating through a separate legal entity, a bribe paid by the JV may lead to liability for a member of the JV if the JV is performing services for the member and the bribe is paid with the intention of benefiting that member. However, the existence of a JV entity will not of itself mean that it is 'associated' with any of its members. A bribe paid on behalf of the JV entity by one of its employees or agents will therefore not trigger liability for members of the JV simply by virtue of them benefiting indirectly from the bribe through their investment in or ownership of the JV.

The situation will be different where the JV is conducted through a contractual arrangement. The degree of control that a participant has over that arrangement is likely to be one of the 'relevant circumstances' that would be taken into account in deciding whether a person who paid a bribe in the conduct of the JV business was 'performing services for or on behalf of' a participant in that arrangement. It may be, for example, that an employee of such a participant who has paid a bribe in order to benefit his employer is not to be regarded as a person 'associated' with all the other participants in the JV. Ordinarily, the employee of a participant will be presumed to be a person performing services for and on behalf of his employer. Likewise, an agent engaged by a participant in a contractual JV is likely to be regarded as a person associated with that participant in the absence of evidence that the agent is acting on behalf of the contractual JV as a whole.

IV.   Procedures

Maintaining a consistent theme throughout this Guidance on the Six Principles of Adequate Procedures anti-bribery program, it is incumbent that a company's due diligence procedures should be proportionate to the identified risk. Due diligence should be conducted using a risk-based approach. For example, in lower risk situations, companies may decide that there is no need to conduct much in the way of due diligence. In higher risk situations, due diligence may include conducting direct interrogative enquiries, indirect investigations, or general research on proposed associated persons.

However, the appropriate level of due diligence to prevent bribery will vary enormously depending on the risks arising from the particular relationship. So, for example, the appropriate level of due diligence required by a company when contracting for the performance of Information Technology (IT) services may be low, to reflect low risks of bribery on its behalf. Conversely, a business entering into the international energy market and selecting an intermediary to assist in establishing a business in such markets will typically require a much higher level of due diligence to mitigate the risks of bribery on its behalf.

One company, The Risk Advisory Group, has put together a handy chart of its Level One, Two and Three approaches to integrity and due diligence. I have found it useful in explaining the different scopes and focuses of the various levels of due diligence.

Level	Issues Addressed	Scope of Investigation
One	• That the company exists • Identities of directors and shareholders • Whether such persons are on regulators' watch lists • Signs that such persons are government officials • Obvious signs	• Company registration and status • Registered Address • Regulators' watch lists • Credit Checks • Bankruptcy/Liquidation Proceedings • Review accounts and auditors comments • Litigation search • Negative media search

	of financial difficulty • Signs of involvement in litigation • Media reports linking the company to corruption	
Two	As above with the following additions: • Public Profile integrity checks • Signs of official investigations and/or sanctions from regulatory authorities • Other anti-corruption Red Flags	As above with the following additions: • Review and summary of all media and internet references • Review and summary of relevant corporate records and litigation filings, including local archives • Analysis and cross-referencing of all findings
Three	As above with the following additions: • But seeking fuller answers to any questions raised by drawing on a wider range of intelligence sources and/or addressing specific issues	As above with the following additions: • Enquiries via local sources • Enquiries via industry experts • Enquiries via western agencies such as embassies or trade promotion bodies • Enquires via sources close to local regulatory

	of potential concern already identified	agencies

The Guidance suggests that more information is likely to be required from companies than from individuals because on a basic level more individuals are likely to be involved in the performance of services by a company and the exact nature of the roles of such individuals or other connected bodies may not be immediately obvious. Therefore a business seeking to retain another company as a business partner should engage in greater due diligence such as through direct requests for details on the background, expertise and business experience, of relevant individuals. Continued monitoring is also suggested, rather than simply annually or bi-annually.

So what's the message from Henry IV? It is to soldier on, keep the faith that your son will eventually grow up and to keep your head about you. Principle IV of Adequate Procedures would seem to call for the same patient work. You should identify those parties that you need to investigate from an anti-bribery perspective, risk rank them and then perform the appropriate level of due diligence.

Principle V - Communication (including training): Henry V and Principle V of the Six Principles of Adequate Procedures: Communication

Posted May 3, 2012

Henry V is a truly inspiring play. Whether one sees it on the stage or on the big screen with the 1944 Olivier or 1989 Brannagh version, one cannot help but draw inspiration about the story of the former Prince Hal, from Henry IV, who becomes a regal monarch and leads the English army to a defeat of the French at the Battle of Agincourt. One of the things that Henry V does extraordinarily well is communicate; about his goals and rousing his subjects to help achieve them. Today we use the prism of Henry V to look at Principle V of the Six Principles of Adequate Procedures; that being "Communication (including training)".

I.   *Commentary*

The Guidance for the Six Principles of Adequate Procedures, anti-bribery program states in Principle V that *"The business seeks to ensure that its bribery prevention policies and procedures are embedded and understood throughout the company through internal and external communication, including training, that is proportionate to the risks it faces."* The Guidance recognizes that communication and training deters bribery by companies, their employees and those persons associated with it, by enhancing awareness and understanding anti-corruption policies and procedures and the company's commitment to their proper application. It therefore follows that making information available on legal requirements and obligations and policies and procedures for implementation of the same assists in more effective monitoring, evaluation and review of bribery prevention procedures. Anti-bribery training should provide, to company employees and those persons and entities associated with the company, the knowledge and skills needed to implement and utilize the anti-bribery procedures and handle in a satisfactory manner any bribery related problems or issues that may arise.

II.   Communication

The Guidance begins by recognizing that the content, language and tone of communications for internal consumption may vary from external use in response to the different relationship the audience has with the company. Further, the nature of communication will vary enormously between businesses in accordance with the different bribery risks faced, the size of the business and the scale and nature of its activities.

1. Internal Communications

It all starts with 'tone from the top' but communications within a business need to also focus on the implementation of the company's anti-bribery policies and procedures. The Guidance lists several areas which it believes such communication should provide instruction upon. These include company policies on "decision making, financial control, hospitality and promotional expenditure, facilitation payments, training, charitable and political donations, penalties for breach of rules and the articulation of management roles at different levels." Another critical aspect of internal communications is the establishment of an ethics helpline. Such a helpline should be secure, confidential and accessible for both employees and those outside the company to elevate concerns about bribery on the part of associated persons, to provide suggestions for improvement of bribery prevention procedures and controls and for requesting advice. The Guidance calls such a tool a "Speak-Up Line" but whatever name it is given, it is clear that those both inside and outside a company need to be furnished with a secure, confidential and safe manner to report ethical concerns to an appropriate level of management.

2. External Communications

Just as risk assessment and due diligence on third parties form a critical component of an Adequate Procedures based anti-bribery corruption program, the Guidance also speaks to the need for external communication of bribery prevention policies through a statement or Code of Conduct, which should act as a deterrent to those intending to bribe on a business's behalf. The Guidance relates that external communications can include information on bribery prevention procedures and controls, sanctions, results of internal surveys, rules governing recruitment, procurement and tendering. The Guidance also recognizes that businesses may consider it proportionate and appropriate to communicate its anti-bribery policies and commitment to a wider audience, such as other companies in their sector, trade association members and to organizations that would fall outside the scope of the range of its associated persons, or to the general public.

III.   *Training*

Restating again that the number one key to an Adequate Procedures anti-bribery compliance program, a company should develop its training protocol based upon a risk assessment. The Guidance recognizes that all employees should receive some training which is likely to be effective in firmly establishing an anti-bribery culture whatever the level of risk. This general level of training can be centered on raising employee awareness about the threats posed by bribery in general and in the industry in which the company operates in particular, and the various ways it is being addressed.

There should be mandatory, general training for new employees or for agents (on a weighted risk basis) as part of the employee indoctrination process, but it should also be tailored to the specific risks associated with specific posts. The Guidance indicates that a company should tailor its training to the special needs of those involved in any procedures and higher risk functions such as purchasing, contracting, distribution, marketing, and those working in high risk countries. It is important to note that for training to be effective it should be continuous, regularly monitored and evaluated.

The Guidance also suggests that associated persons undergo training. This will be particularly relevant for high risk associated persons. The better practice is to require such anti-bribery training as a part of compliance contractual terms and conditions and then provide such training to the highest risk third party representatives. But the Guidance does recognize that a company may wish to encourage associated persons to adopt bribery prevention training. If this is done, the training should be evaluated and appropriate records of business partner training be submitted to the company on no less than an annual basis.

The Guidance also recognizes that there are various media which can be used to deliver training. It lists some of the different training formats which are available in addition to the traditional classroom or seminar formats, such as e-learning and other web-based tools. However, a company should not lose sight of a risk based approach, so that those employees or third parties deemed the highest risk need to receive the most intensive training. Finally, whatever the format of the anti-bribery training, it should seek to achieve its objective of ensuring that those participating in it develop a firm understanding of what the relevant policies and procedures mean in practice for them.

So how can you channel Henry V to help your compliance program? Perhaps you could begin by re-reading the play or some of its most inspiring scenes or even watching them on You Tube. You can start with the St. Crispin's Day Speech, ride once more into the breach, or even the Prologue to learn about communication.

Principle VI - Monitoring and Review: Sherlock Holmes and Principle 6 of an Adequate Procedures Compliance Program

Posted April 20, 2012

I am a big fan of Sherlock Holmes, on radio, television and the movies but particularly in print. Last summer I re-read the Doyle collection and it was like revisiting an old friend. So today, we celebrate the story of the *"The Six Napoleons"*. In this story, an apparent thief is breaking into private residences and commercial establishments to seemingly smash statuettes of Napoleon. While the slow thinking police think that a rabid Francophobe is terrorizing the Francophiles of London, Holmes sees something very different and indeed much more sinister. It turns out that a very hot, stolen jewel was hidden in one statue, many of which were then sold so the jewel thief has to find the correct statuette to find the stolen jewel. Holmes, of course, deduces this and catches the thief.

This leads into the conclusion of my series on the Six Principles of Adequate Procedures under the UK Bribery Act; with Principle VI - Monitoring and Review. This Principle recognizes that a company should monitor and review its anti-bribery and anti-corruption procedures designed to prevent bribery by persons associated with it and make improvements where necessary. Indeed the Guidance from the UK Ministry of Justice (MOJ) relates that *"The bribery risks that a commercial organisation faces may change over time, as may the nature and scale of its activities, so the procedures required to mitigate those risks are also likely to change. Commercial organisations will therefore wish to consider how to monitor and evaluate the effectiveness of their bribery prevention procedures and adapt them where necessary. In addition to regular monitoring, an organisation might want to review its processes in response to other stimuli, for example governmental changes in countries in which they operate, an incident of bribery or negative press reports."*

Generally, I believe there are two strategic reasons to follow Principle VI of the Guidance. The first is that the only way to know if your compliance program is effective is to test it. The second is that changes in your business model, market conditions, legislation or other external events could increase your anti-bribery and anti-corruption compliance risk well beyond the risks that your compliance regime was intended to manage when it was initially designed and implemented. I find that a compliance assessment is becoming of greater importance to achieve a minimum *best practices* compliance program. Representatives of the US Department of Justice (DOJ) talk about such a concept in terms of a risk assessment but the precepts are the same. A company needs to assess its program and its effectiveness on a regular basis so that it does not become stale.

Procedures

The Guidance recognizes that there are a wide range of internal and external review mechanisms available for a company to use when assessing its compliance program. As for ongoing evaluation of effectiveness, the Guidance notes that "systems set up to deter, detect and investigate bribery, and monitor the ethical quality of transactions, such as internal financial control mechanisms, will help provide insight into the effectiveness of procedures designed to prevent bribery." Some of the specific techniques which can be used include staff surveys, questionnaires and feedback from training. All of these can also provide an important source of information on effectiveness and a means by which employees and other associated persons can inform continuing improvement of anti-bribery policies. Continuous controls monitoring is becoming another tool for companies to use in their ongoing compliance program. Witness the recent statements by the DOJ in its declination to prosecute Morgan Stanley for the acts of its former Managing Director, Garth Peterson.

The Guidance also speaks to more formal periodic reviews and reports for top-level management. I would suggest that an annual risk assessment is one mechanism which should be used by companies. The Guidance further suggests that businesses could also draw on information on other similarly situated company's *best practices*, for example relevant trade bodies or regulators might highlight examples of good or bad practice in their publications. Once again the DOJ has provided solid guidance in this area by listing several of the areas in which it believes that a company should assess its anti-bribery and anti-corruption risks. These include: (1) Geography - Where does your Company do business?; (2) Interaction with types and levels of Governments; (3) Industrial Sector of Operations; (4) Involvement with Joint Ventures; (5) Licenses and Permits in Operations; (6) Degree of Government Oversight and (7) Volume and Importance of Goods and Personnel Going Through Customs and Immigration. In addition to using this information to inform your compliance program, your company can also use such information to update its compliance program in today's ever changing business environment.

Lastly, the Guidance directs that companies should also avail themselves of some form of external verification or assurance of the effectiveness of anti-bribery procedures. The Guidance says that "*Some organisations may be able to apply for certified compliance with one of the independently-verified anti-bribery standards maintained by industrial sector associations or multilateral bodies. However, such certification may not necessarily mean that a commercial organisation's bribery prevention procedures are 'adequate' for all purposes where an offence under section 7 of the Bribery Act could be charged.*" While there are no universally recognized standards that I am aware, many third parties can come in and perform an independent assessment of a company's overall compliance program.

So we end our series on the Six Principles of Adequate Procedures anti-bribery and anti-corruption compliance program with this memorable quote from the Sherlock Holmes story *"The Sign of Four"*, *"How often have I said to you that when you have eliminated the impossible, whatever remains, however improbable, must be the truth?"* This would seem to place the exclamation point on Principle VI; if you fairly and adequately assess your compliance program, you can not only determine its effectiveness but also help to enhance your compliance regime going forward.

B. General

Inbound Corruption and the UK Bribery Act

Posted July 6, 2011

The UK Bribery Act, as hopefully everyone is aware by now, became effective last Friday, July 1. Most compliance practitioners are keenly aware of its application to UK based companies or subsidiaries for bribery of governmental officials and private parties. Many companies have understood that these types of activities are illegal under the Foreign Corrupt Practices Act (FCPA) in connection with foreign governments and foreign governmental officials and some companies focused on these types of schemes when they involve private, non-governmental actors. However, the Bribery Act prohibitions apply to inbound schemes that involve bribery as well. These include bribery of a UK company or subsidiary's employees. Most companies focus on the outbound schemes so we thought it might be a propitious time to review the different types of fraud schemes that that might be covered by the Bribery Act for inbound actions.

In her book *"Expert Fraud Investigation: A Step-By-Step Guide"* Tracy Coenen details several types of fraud investigations. In addition to the book as a useful tool for the fraud examiner, Coenen also provides the lay person with a general discussion of the types of corruption schemes a company may face and how best to prevent them. As well as outright bribery there are several types of inbound corruption; including kickbacks, extortion, conflict of interests, and related party transactions as examples of corruption which can involve a payment to obtain an advantage, receive preferential treatment, or force certain preferential actions.

Kickbacks

Kickbacks occur when a company overpays for goods or services and then remits all or part of the overpaid amount back to the perpetrator. This can be affected by the person in charge of the overall bidding process. However, it can extend down into any other employees involved in the approval process such as employees in production, engineering or quality control. So, similar to bribery, there can be more subtle forms of kickbacks and such forms can include the substitution of inferior components into an overall product while charging the higher price to the end-user/purchaser. Kickbacks can also include irregularities in pricing and quality throughout a project. Even if inferior quality goods are not substituted, an irregular price can inflate the cost of goods paid for by a company.

Extortion

Extortion is in many ways the mirror image of bribery. Whereas with a bribe, something of value is given to obtain a benefit, with extortion, a payment is demanded. While such demand can be made to obtain a benefit, such as to allow a company to go forward in a bidding process; extortion can also be made to prevent injuries to persons and damage to physical facilities. While not nearly as common as bribes, there are cases where extortions have been made and money paid based upon the threats.

Conflict of Interest

Many people do not think of conflicts of interest when considering a corruption scheme. Nevertheless, if an employee, executive, or owner of a company has an undisclosed interest in an entity with which his company is doing business, the situation can present a conflict of interest. In the conflict of interest scheme, the employee, executive, or owner may be able to influence the company decision making process in order to send business to the other entity. This conflict of interest may be broader than simply directly involving an employee, executive or owner; it can extend to wives, children and other family members who stand to benefit from any such undisclosed interest.

Related Third Party Transactions

Many compliance practitioners do not consider transactions with third parties as part of an overall fraud scheme. However, if the third party transactions are not conducted in an arms-length manner, this may well be indicia of an overall fraud scheme. Problems can arise when the related parties have a special advantage in doing business with a company and when that special advantage harms the company through increased costs, decreased revenue or other concessions.

In addition to the types of schemes listed in the categories above, Coenen lists several different types of such transactions. They include:

- Extending credit to a company which would not otherwise be so entitled;
- Writing off accounts receivables with no legitimate business reason;
- Doing business with a small or one-man shop with no physical assets or simply a post office box for an office;
- Engaging in consulting agreements where no substantive work is done for payments received;
- A consultant who engages in extensive 'market research' in foreign countries with little to no tangible work product; and

- Concealing the existence of direct or indirect ownership in entities with which a company is doing business.

So what can a company to do combat inbound bribery and corruption? The techniques will be familiar to the compliance practitioner; they include ongoing monitoring programs of both accounts and transactions, through robust internal controls. It is also recommended that there be an anonymous reporting hotline through which employees can alert management of such activities without fear of supervisor retaliation. However, the most important form is that management set the correct "Tone at the Top" that such fraudulent activity within the company will not be tolerated.

What are the differences in the FCPA and Bribery Act?

Posted March 3, 2011

Yesterday in a post entitled *"The Shrinking UK Bribery Act"* the FCPA Professor discussed some of the information coming out of the UK regarding how the Bribery Act may be interpreted. He stated that it appears that the UK Serious Fraud Office (SFO) will not implement the full ban on facilitation payments and will apply a reasonableness standard for gifts, entertainment and travel expenses, although no such standard is built into the Bribery Act itself. New Ministry of Justice (MOJ) guidance may also give a company some protection against corrupt acts by a joint venture (JV) partner. He stated that he believes at the end of the day, "the Bribery Act will look very much like the FCPA. In fact, because of the Bribery Act's adequate procedures defense and other hinted at limitations, the Bribery Act may turn out to be more lenient than the FCPA."

With the recent information coming out, largely from reports by the UK newspaper The Telegraph, we thought it might a propitious time to review the differences in the Bribery Act and the Foreign Corrupt Practices Act (FCPA) so that US companies might begin to plan to acclimate their FCPA based compliance program to one which includes concepts found in the Bribery Act, if such action is appropriate.

With that in mind we were pleased when we saw that our colleague Michael Whitener, of Vista Law, had put together a handy chart comparing the two laws. With Michael's permission we reprint his summary comparison below.

US FCPA vs. UK BRIBERY ACT

Provision	FCPA	Bribery Act
Who is being bribed	Only bribes ("anything of value") paid or offered to a "foreign official" are prohibited	Prohibits bribes paid to *any person* to induce them to act "improperly" (not limited to foreign officials)
Nature of advantage obtained	Payment must be "to obtain or retain business"	Focus is on improper action rather than business nexus (except in case of strict corporate liability)
"Active offense" vs. "passive offense"	Only the act of payment, rather than the receipt/acceptance of payment, is prohibited	Creates two offenses: (1) offense of bribing another ("active offense") and (2) offense of being bribed ("passive offense")
Corporate strict liability	Strict liability only under accounting provisions for public companies (failure to maintain adequate systems of internal controls)	Creates a new strict liability corporate offense for the failure of a commercial organization to prevent bribery (subject to defense of having "adequate procedures" in place designed to prevent bribery)

Jurisdiction	U.S. companies and citizens, foreign companies listed on U.S. stock exchange, or any person acting while in the U.S.	Individuals who are UK nationals or are ordinarily resident in the UK and organizations that are either established in the UK or conduct some part of their business in the UK
Business promotion expenditures	Affirmative defense for reasonable and bona fide expenditure directly related to the business promotion or contract performance	No similar defense (but arguably such expenditures are not "improper" and therefore not a Bribery Act violation)
Allowable under local law	Affirmative defense if payment is lawful under written laws/regulations of foreign country	No violation if permissible under written laws of foreign country (applies only in case of bribery of foreign public official; otherwise a factor to be considered)
Facilitating payments	Exception for payment to a foreign official to expedite or secure the performance of a routine (non-discretionary) government action	No facilitating payments exception, although guidance is likely to provide that payments of small amounts of money are unlikely to be prosecuted

	Both civil and criminal proceedings can be brought by DOJ and SEC	Criminal enforcement only by the UK Serious Fraud Office (SFO)
Civil/criminal enforcement	Both civil and criminal proceedings can be brought by DOJ and SEC	Criminal enforcement only by the UK Serious Fraud Office (SFO)
Potential penalties	Bribery: for individuals, up to five years' imprisonment and fines of up to $250,000; for entities, fines of up to $2 million Books and records/internal control violations: for individuals, up to 20 year's imprisonment and fines of up $5 million; for entities, fines of up to $25 million	For individuals, up to 10 years' imprisonment and potentially unlimited fines; for entities, potentially unlimited fines

We still believe that all US companies which have a UK subsidiary or do business in the UK need to be cognizant of the requirements of the Bribery Act. Each company should review its own compliance policy to determine if changes need to be made to bring their compliance program into compliance with the Bribery Act. This summary chart is an excellent tool for setting out the differences and allowing a US company to more easily assess where it may need to make changes. We commend Michael for putting this chart together and for making it available to us for this post.

Preparing for the End of Facilitation Payments

Posted September 15, 2011

In an article published in the July issue of the Compliance Week magazine, entitled *"The UK Bribery Act"*, authors Jonathan Feig and Richard Thomas discuss how companies can mitigate their risks of prosecution for making facilitation payments under the Bribery Act. This is an area that many US companies may have exposure to as the Foreign Corrupt Practices Act (FCPA) has an exception for facilitation payments but there is no corresponding exception or exemption under the Bribery Act.

Richard Alderman, Director of the Serious Fraud Office (SFO), was recently quoted in *thebriberyact.com* regarding facilitation payments as saying:

> "...I do not expect facilitation payments to end the moment the Bribery Act comes into force. What I do expect though is for corporates who do not yet have a zero tolerance approach to these payments, to commit themselves to such an approach and to work on how to eliminate these payments over a period of time. I have also said that these corporates should come and talk to the SFO about these issues so that we can understand that their commitment is real. This also gives the corporate the opportunity to talk to us about the problems that they face in carrying on business in the areas in which they trade. It is important for us to know this in order to discuss with the corporate what is a *sensible process*." [*emphasis mine*]

As a lawyer, you might well seek further clarification on what the "sensible approach" might be and how one could advise a client on such a term. Fortunately that is exactly what my colleagues who run *thebriberyact.com* did. Richard Kovalevsky QC and Barry Vitou sought further guidance from the SFO and reported that the SFO will be "looking to see" the following:

1. Whether the company has a clear issued policy regarding such payments;
2. Whether written guidance is available to relevant employees as to the procedure they should follow when asked to make such payments;
3. Whether such procedures are being followed by employees;
4. If there is evidence that all such payments are being recorded by the company;
5. If there is evidence that proper action (collective or otherwise) is being taken to inform the appropriate authorities in the countries concerned that such payments are being demanded;
6. Whether the company is taking what practical steps it can to curtail the making of such payments.

If the answers to these questions are satisfactory then the corporate should be shielded from prosecution. The Feig and Thomas article would seem to speak to this final Point 6, what practical steps is your company taking "to curtail the making of such [facilitation] payments"? They lay out a 5 step process to help curtail the making of facilitation payments.

I. Revisit the Anti-Corruption Policy

Your company should have a plan to phase out facilitation payments made by both company employees and those working on your behalf such as agents, resellers, distributor and other foreign business partners.

II. Understand How Operations Have Changed Since the Ban on Facilitation Payments

Your company should consider key areas where facilitation payments occur to make certain that they are not being paid in another form. For instance, do employees wait in line like everyone else to go through customs or do they now use an agent to shuffle them through in groups. If your company has engaged in such a customs representative, has this agent been vetted through your due diligence program and if so has this agent been audited?

III. Understand How Employees Manage Situations Where They are Pressured to Make Facilitation Payments

The key here is listening. Your company needs to listen to key employees who travel overseas to high risk areas about situations that they face where a bribe is solicited. Your company also needs an understanding of areas where what employees face is not solicitation of bribes but really extortion because their life, liberty or health and safety is in immediate peril. Your company will back them up if they are required to pay monies to extricate themselves from such a situation.

IV. Update Training and Internal Communications for Facilitation Payments

Your company must update your training to make clear that facilitation payments will no longer be allowed under your compliance program. The information that your company obtains from listening to your employees, as set out above will enable your company to develop information that they will need for situations where a bribe is demanded. Incorporating the likely scenarios that employees will face into your training is important so that your company can present responses which can be used by employees. This way an employee is not left out in the cold or in the dark about what might happen and what he or she can do about it.

V. Update Your Anti-Corruption Monitoring Program

Your company should update its anti-corruption monitoring program to ensure that it captures the identification of facilitation payments. If any such payments are identified, they should be elevated to the compliance department. These controls need to be tested to ascertain their effectiveness. Lastly, such controls need to be extended to your foreign business partners.

As I have previously written, the end of facilitation payments in coming. The OECD recommends that they be done away with and the Bribery Act provides no exemption for them. Perhaps a Republican Congress would feel that by removing the facilitation payment exemption it would somehow hurt US businesses overseas. But this feeling would not last for long. So if your company does business in the UK or has a UK subsidiary, you need to start preparing for the end of facilitation payments. You would do well to regularly read *thebriberyact.com* and to follow the steps laid out by Feig and Thomas in the Compliance Week magazine.

Letter from England: The Bribery Act Guys and the Act's US Implications

Posted August 5, 2011

Earlier this week I had the opportunity to sit down and lunch with Barry Vitou and Richard Kovalevsky, QC, authors of the website *thebriberyact.com*. A great time was certainly had by all and in honor of their website and the venue; I enjoyed a fine meal of fish and chips.

The two are a great pair, with Barry a solicitor and Richard a barrister (hence the omnipresent 'QC' after his name). One of the things I was interested in was how these two came to the field of anti-corruption and how they came to start up such a focused, and maintain what I believe to be the best, and comprehensive website for information on the UK Bribery Act, and other anti-bribery and anti-corruption news across the globe. Back in 2009 they began to follow the legislative meanderings for the Bribery Act and decided to start a website to highlight the legislation and bring commentary and analysis to the Bribery Bill as it worked its way through Parliament and to the Bribery Act after it received its Royal Assent.

From my perspective, the site has been an excellent resource for the US compliance practitioner. As I previously wrote their commentary and analysis is insightful and cuts much of the speculation about the reach and over-reach of the Act. They blog about concrete topics and issues and provide to the compliance practitioner useful guidance on how to implement or enhance a compliance program to comply with the strictures of the Act. However, for my money, the one thing that makes their website stand out is the interviews they have provided of UK officials charged with implementing the Act. These interviews provide, not only awareness into the thinking of the very highest level of UK officials but, more importantly, they allow the US compliance practitioner to read and inform his or her own views of how the Act will be implemented going forward.

One of the areas we discussed was US companies and their implementation of Bribery Act compliance programs or enhancing their Foreign Corrupt Practices Act (FCPA) based compliance programs to incorporate the requirements of the Bribery Act. One area which I do not see significant thought or compliance program enhancement for is regarding the fact that under the Bribery Act, the US is a foreign jurisdiction, therefore all the requirements of the Act come into play in transactions in the US.

Most US companies do not subject their US sales channel, whether they are sales agents, representatives, distributors or others, to the same type of compliance due diligence that is required of their sales channel outside the US. The same is true for vendors in the supply chain; a Dun & Bradstreet credit worthiness report may be all the investigation that they do.

The same lack of process and procedure is true for other components of the Six Principles of Adequate Procedures compliance regime. There is no compliance training required of US based sales channel or supply chain, no requirement for ongoing compliance assessment or evaluation, no requirement for a like or similar overall company compliance program, no requirement of risk assessment or ongoing monitoring or review. In short the vast majority of US companies do not meet the standards of Adequate Procedures of the Bribery Act when looking at the companies they do business with, both ingoing and outgoing in the US.

As our lunch was winding down I told both Richard and Barry one thing was definitely, and certainly, required and that was that they come to the US and put on Bribery Act events across the US. They somewhat blushed when I told them that the *Bribery Act Guys on Tour* would be quite successful and many, many of my fellow compliance practitioners would certainly benefit from their collective wit and wisdom. I know I would.

INDEX

A

B

C

D

T

U

V

W

39356476R00142

Made in the USA
Lexington, KY
19 February 2015